a woman's shed

a woman's shed

spaces for women to create, write, make, grow, think, and escape

Gill Heriz

with photography by
Nicolette Hallett

CICO BOOKS
LONDON NEW YORK

For Sam and Tora

This book is dedicated to all women who create sheds, but particularly to one woman for whom sheds are her lifeblood and who was the inspiration for the birth of this celebration. Lizzy Smith has, over the years, built sheds wherever she has lived as surely as the shoots of spring are impelled to rise, bringing forth the promise of extraordinary creations. There have been corrugated iron structures, humble tool sheds, saunas, and leviathan boat sheds. As we celebrate these private spaces, I recognize that the seeds of recording that celebration were sown with this eccentric shed-woman.

Published in 2014 by CICO Books
An imprint of Ryland Peters & Small Ltd
20–21 Jockey's Fields, London WC1R 4BW
519 Broadway, 5th Floor, New York, NY 10012

www.rylandpeters.com

10 9 8 7 6 5 4 3 2 1

Text © Gill Heriz 2014
Design and photography © CICO Books 2014

A CIP catalog record for this book is available from the Library of Congress and the British Library.

ISBN: 978 1 78249 099 9

Printed in China

Editor: Helen Ridge
Designer: Alison Fenton
Photographers: all photography by Nicolette Hallett, except pp. 116-117 (Gill Heriz), pp. 124-125 (Trish le Gal), pp.30-31 and 186-187 (Tracy Litterick), and p. 134 (Lindsay Simon).

For digital editions, visit
www.cicobooks.com/apps.php

Contents

What is it about sheds that is so appealing?

Do they remind us of the hiding places, of our childhood, when we made dens out of anything and everything, wherever we could, turning bunk beds, packing cases, ruined walls, and hedges into our own secret places, and lost ourselves in the world of our imagination?

As we sit in our centrally heated houses, amid the trappings of consumerism, do we, as adults, crave that simpler life? Is there a collective primal memory of a more elemental existence that gives us direct contact with the few things we need in order to live? When we enter our sheds, we see a table, a chair, a bench, boxes of tools, seeds, a simple stove, a tea kettle. We can pretend, play, create, be ourselves, and find freedom from the paraphernalia of everyday contemporary life.

When we were young we tried to understand the mystery of our fathers disappearing into their sheds, their own private realms, but as girls then, and as women now, we, too, have built, converted, and kitted out spaces for our own needs away from everyday life. Women, too, have sheds.

When the idea for this book arose, I keyed in the words "Women's Sheds" on the internet, which led to the digital universe scratching its patriarchal head. The initial response was that "shed" meant losing weight. A second attempt brought the reply, "Do you mean 'Men's Sheds?'" No, I did not! I tried again. There was more scrunching of the massive labyrinthine lexicon wrapped around the whole of our e-planet and reaching into the stars. "Do you mean 'Women's Shoes?'"

The invisibility of women's sheds began to raise a challenge. Are women's private and working spaces meant to be invisible? Are they so private that we succeed in hiding them from the rest of the world? Do we enjoy the assumption that sheds are for men, and thin women like shoes a lot?

In the West, for the last two hundred years or so, women have been primarily identified as "homemakers," even when they have also been engaged in paid work outside the home. Women have snatched moments and spaces for their own creativity, while dealing with the demands of everyday domestic and working lives. Nevertheless, in this context, "the shed" has been a sanctuary for men to "retreat" to or for women to be "banned" from. Thus the shed has never been known as a space for women. It has been seen as a non-domestic male space for male activities—absolute privacy away from the female domain.

Women as gardeners may be the exception to this generalization but what's certain is that, historically, women have built, bought, and converted spaces for themselves for a whole variety of reasons and for a wide range of uses. And they still are.

above Aileen's shed was her gift to herself when her father left her some money.

Traditionally, women have taken time for moments of creativity within their demanding everyday lives wherever they could. They have always used small domestic spaces, and that sometimes included sheds, for their own practical and creative needs. These humble or not so humble sheds have, undoubtedly, been the places for inspiration, for the creation of novels, paintings, and the making of gardens.

Going to the shed is both a physical removal of ourselves to "another place," and a retreat to a space where our emotional needs are met and we can be ourselves. Our sheds are often the one place we can call our own and where we can do what we like!

In our sheds we create art, we write or make cartoons, and reach out to the world through doing the things we enjoy and which challenge us. We plant seeds, retreat, think, work, make, and mend, and have the tools of our trade around us. We collect curios and turn detritus into art. We gather totems from walks, vacations, and loves, and then artfully enshrine them or carelessly allow them to collect cobwebs on windowsills. We store spades, brushes, memories, and chitting potatoes.

For many women in this book, the link to nature, to the sounds and sights of birds, insects, and animals through windows and doors thrown open is at the

above Lizzy has built several sheds for her friends, but this is the latest one that she built for herself.

heart of their enjoyment of their sheds. Many describe the owls, the pheasant, the wren... as well as the sounds from inside of mice nesting and the shed itself creaking with a life of its own.

This book is an exploration through fields and gardens, around corners, and down intriguing paths to find visions of sheds and spaces created anew or re-invented by women for themselves. Sometimes they are magnificent in their ambition and grandeur, sometimes tumbledown, utilitarian, and ordinary. They are built from timber, tin, brick, adobe; they are huge and they are tiny. Then there are the women for whom one shed is simply not enough.

This journey takes us to sheds from the U.S. and the U.K, from France and beyond. It is a very eclectic collection, with different visions, uses, and materials. Some are designed for beauty, while others evolve for purely practical reasons. Whether you have a shed or not, you will find inspiration in these pages.

As we travel, we are guided by themes such as vision, sense of place, use of space, memories, creativity, and resources. There is no intention for those themes to be rigid or to define each shed. A shed may be a place of creativity and hold memories, be a retreat and a place of work, for instance. Indeed, our spaces can perform many functions and meet many of our needs. The best sheds do this!

It is hard to give coherence to the sometimes multiple uses that women have for their sheds. Themes, however, do emerge, and we have divided this book into seven chapters.

The best-known sheds, and possibly the most ancient, are those of growers—gardeners, plantswomen, women who keep animals, and farmers. They need a place to store tools, seeds, and animal feed, and somewhere to provide shelter from the rain or the sun, somewhere to sit, sort seeds, or do nothing. Occasionally, the garden shed starts to become a mini-home with armchairs, paintings, a stove, tea, and eggs.

We look at the arts in three sections: the sculptors and potters, the painters, and the makers. All these women use the tools of their trade to bring to life the products of their creative imaginations and labors.

Then there are those women who have built their own sheds—or imagined and dreamed their sheds into being with the help of others. We look at what inspired them and how they did it, the materials used, and the concepts of recycling, re-inventing, and re-using.

Women working from home use their sheds as an office space, with a desk for planning, thinking, writing, and creating. In the face of the continuing dual responsibilities for earning money and domestic life, this is the "go-to-work" place, giving us the separate space we need. There is flexibility as well as some level of control over whom we allow into our sheds.

Then I write about what sheds have to do with our lifestyles and how we live. The shed can be an extra bedroom for guests or visiting family, somewhere close but offering a little independence. We may also sleep there ourselves from time to time, enjoying the simplicity of being away from the clutter and machinery of the house.

For a few women their shed is also their permanent home. They may have downsized or just prefer to live simply, whether for economic, environmental, or personal reasons. And then sheds can be the repositories of the stuff of living, from boats, blankets, and baskets to tents and anything we don't want to keep in the house but can't bring ourselves to get rid of.

Many women and their sheds resist being categorized, and some may have many sheds for different reasons and uses. These are located in the chapter where they most reflect the women themselves. These hard-to-define sheds may be complex but they are always interesting—just like the women who own them.

My hope in writing this book is that the spirit of all these women and their sheds comes through, whether they are beach huts, trailers (caravans), shacks, garden sheds, barns, lean-tos, falling down promises of sheds-to-be, or magnificent tailor-made constructions.

There will be some who will ask 'Is this really a shed?' To answer that, in the panel above there are some definitions, and the approach taken for this book.

What is a shed?

Can we describe any building which is separate from the main building as a "shed?". Here are some definitions:

Chambers Dictionary says that a shed is "a structure, often open fronted, for storing or shelter; an outhouse."

A **Thesaurus** comes up with the words hut, lean-to, shack, tool shed, bicycle shed.

Wikipedia says that "a shed is typically a simple, single-story structure in a back garden or on an allotment that is used for storage, hobbies, or as a workshop," and that "sheds vary considerably in the complexity of their construction and their size, from small open-sided tin-roofed structures to large wood-framed sheds with shingled roofs, windows, and electrical outlets."

The word "shed" is thought to derive from Scead, which is an Anglo-Saxon word meaning shade. Sheds were therefore functional rather than aesthetic structures.

In the end we find that each shed has a different meaning for each woman. So we asked the women themselves to talk to us about their own sheds, and what they mean to them.

Chapter 1

Sheds **for painters**

Painters have made their marks on surfaces throughout time and across continents. Using their imagination, they have transformed paper, canvas, any surface you can imagine, through line, form, and color. Styles are from the decorative to the political; from the figurative to the abstract. Culture, styles, and practices give us a myriad distinctive works of such variety that there is something for everyone to relate to or be inspired by.

Women's sheds and studios provide environments for a rich variety of expression. Inspiration might start in the imagination; in the landscape; in the market place; from photographs and multi-layered sketch books exploring nature, relationships, the world, and ourselves.

Painters' sheds or studios are places of alchemy: paints, brushes, bottles and jars, the smells of white spirit and oils, of pastels and chalk. There are the sounds of the radio, of a hammer and nails... the unrolling of canvas or laying out of paper... color waiting to be formed into art.

There are the ubiquitous arguments and discussions about art, what it is, and whether it has value. But one thing is certain—it is all around us, and much of it has been made in women's sheds.

Covered in clematis, jasmine, and roses, this wooden hut is almost invisible and in a world of its own. To reach it, **Alison** has to pass under a metal arch of climbers, which flower until the frost comes along. In summer, the hut is completely hidden from the house, which is situated in Blakeney, Norfolk, England. The hut is Alison's studio, where she not only paints but, more important, gives herself time to imagine, with Theo the cat by her side.

above Alison's hut is almost hidden from view, tucked away at the end of the garden.

opposite The hand-operated etching press is used to make different types of artists' prints. Its glass top belonged to an old Morris Minor car.

inset Framing the door is a tangle of climbing clematis, jasmine, and roses, held up by a metal arch. Their heady perfume wafts into the hut in summer.

The hut is a tidy jumble. Well, maybe not so tidy but one senses that everything has its place, even though, to the outsider, there is no apparent order. The placement of seemingly random objects actually has an aesthetic that comes from this artist's creative mind. There are brushes and pens in pots and mugs, shelves of paper, inks and paints.

Alison uses the hand-operated etching press to make artists' prints—etchings, drypoints, and collagraphs—by hand in small editions. The glass top alongside is a recycled windshield from an old Morris Minor car, on which she mixes ink and rolls it out with a brass-handled roller.

The walls are a patchwork of rich brown varnished plywood, except for the "gallery" wall that Alison has painted a pale blue, to create a neutral backdrop and also inject some light into the space when the days are overcast. Pinned haphazardly to it are magazine tear sheets, posters, postcards, photos, scribbles, and small works of art, for both enjoyment and inspiration. Alison loves being outside in the garden (yard) and, when it's sunny, she will take a break from the studio and maybe cuddle the cat. But even when it's wet and windy, she can still enjoy the feeling of the outdoors while tucked away warm and dry in the hut, with the rain beating down rhythmically on the roof and the wind howling all around. When it's hot and she's working at her press, the door remains open and Theo can come and go as he pleases.

"I like that tidying up in the hut is cursory—just making enough space to sit down and get on with something is fine. None of this 'making things hygienic or neat.' And if, in my enthusiasm, I spill paint or glue or drop bits of paper on the floor, who cares? Nobody on their deathbed ever said they wish they'd done more dusting!"

"One visitor said it was the bleakest studio he had seen."

left A jumble of potted plants outside the rather run-down lean-to contrives to make Tessa's studio a little less stark.

below The cool north light is perfect for painting. Works in progress are propped up wherever there is space.

This shed is, in fact, a brick-built lean-to, fitting snugly against a pretty cottage, near Halesworth, Suffolk, England. At a guess, the cottage is about three hundred years old. Pots and troughs of plants stand higgledy-piggledy outside, beneath the two tall windows that let in the cool north light. It's an entirely functional space, with a single room, painted top to toe in white. This acts as a backdrop to **Tessa's** oil paintings of rural scenes. Evidence of her work is everywhere, from the paint stains on the wooden floor to the boxes of oil paints and painting rags. It is a place of work and creativity.

above Whimsical coastal scenes decorate an old wooden box.

Tessa keeps her workspace simple, so that she can focus on whatever she is painting. She knows it's not the most glamorous of studios and, being north-facing, it's also not easy to keep warm, but an old-fashioned, one-bar electric heater does the job. However, it suits her needs perfectly. She has done her painting here for thirty years, and it is where she feels settled, secure, and able to concentrate.

Distractions are few, but the pair of blackbirds that return each year to nest in the bay tree in the backyard are always welcome. Every spring there is a new family to enjoy. When Tessa had her cat, she would often see the birds eating rather brazenly from the cat's dish. Now, it's the miniature dachshund, Nina, who keeps Tessa company, settling herself in front of the heater.

Tessa does most of her drawing from life. She then brings the drawings back to the studio where she paints the scenes in oils on boards previously washed with color. She spends hours completely absorbed in her work, while a classical music station plays on the radio in the background. Whenever she feels like a reviving cup of tea, she returns to the kitchen next door.

Tessa's commute to her shed, from the domestic to the creative, takes just seconds, but her working day actually starts at the breakfast table. Dressed in her painting sweater, she thinks about what she's going to paint for the rest of the day. Last thing at night, just before going to bed, she will revisit her current painting in the shed to take a final look and then sleep on it.

Nicky enjoys the fact that the informal gallery and studio for her paintings, behind her house in Harleston, Suffolk, were originally part of a workshop in a carter's yard. Dating back to around 1876, the long, brick structure was built by a Samuel Borrett, a carter as well as a builder. She even has the beautiful, original, handwritten deeds that list the yard, the workshop, the stable, and a well.

The open yard is entered through large double doors, and its history is there for all to see. The uneven and worn flagstones speak of a distant time when carts and horses were driven over them as they clattered in and out.

Nicky has converted the sheds at the back of the yard into her studio. Ancient nails for holding all those essential lengths of rope and various tools remain hammered into the beams. Everything about the space is makeshift and a bit decrepit. There is a patchwork of glass in the windows, and the door has an extra piece attached to the bottom, to stop the rain from seeping in underneath. The clay lump wall is returning to straw-filled mud where a previous owner tried to paint it with modern latex (emulsion) paint.

Despite all this, Nicky enjoys the space and the separation that her studio gives her from domestic life. It provides her with everything she needs to do her painting. There is a solid floor and a sound roof to keep the water out from above. Electricity has been laid on so there's enough light to work by when the days become shorter. A sink has been plumbed in so she can wash out her brushes.

She loves to watch the resident blackbirds and robins busying themselves just outside. However, come winter, the studio is far too cold and she retreats to her warm and womb-like kitchen in the house to work.

above The building used as the gallery and studio is steeped in history. Dating back to around 1876, it was orginally a workshop in a carter's yard. Nicky is proud to own the original deeds.

opposite, inset The studio has certainly seen better days but it contains everything Nicky needs, from a plumbed-in sink to a floor-standing lamp.

opposite, below Against a backdrop of white-painted brickwork, the gallery display of Nicky's still lifes, painted in oils, is highlighted by an adjustable lamp.

"My shed is my folly. Built to my own design with a glass roof. It's somewhere I can sing if I want to. A little bit of heaven. That is it really. Nothing more complicated than that."

This pretty little studio stands in a hidden corner in the garden (yard) of Ann's bed & breakfast, overlooking the trees of the Waveney valley in Suffolk, England. The setting is so secluded that guests are unable to see it as they breakfast in the conservatory of the house. To reach it, Ann has to weave her way past pots and planters of glorious flowers, interspersed with metalwork garden chairs and tables. **Ann** built the studio as an escape from the demands of her business, and refers to it as her "folly." Here, she enters her own fantasy world, combining photography with paint and print, using the lush flowers around her as inspiration.

Ann is justifiably proud of her shed. Bright with light coming in through the windows as well as the corrugated plastic roof, it has a black and white checkered floor, which acts as a sharp contrast to the colorful textures of her work. The flowers surrounding the shed and those inside are echoed by the paintings, fabrics, and prints that she has created. In fact, the shed contains so much color and foliage that it could be a glasshouse or a conservatory. Ann has even painted a lush landscape on the back wall as a fake vista. Much of the furniture has been painted, too—she has covered the chest of drawers with vignettes from nature, and painted the little chair a pretty peppermint-green.

Sometimes we have high hopes when envisaging the shed we want. **Nicolette** ordered hers online but when it was finally in place by the vegetable patch and the stables, she found it wanting. She did not warm to its alarming green presence, which was in stark contrast to the delightful surroundings, where hens scratch in the soil, horses graze in the paddocks, and fields and hedges stretch out as far as the eye can see.

The shed was put up for Nicolette one winter by an amiable gang of Poles—not an enviable job in the rain and the mud. After it was built, it began to take on a life of its own. It quickly showed a tendency to warp and part with itself. The new wood, tormented by the weather, refused to settle down. Friendly builders later wrestled it into submission and put in a wood-burning stove set upon a stone hearth. At least Nicolette can now use the shed all year round now with efficient heating to keep her warm.

In spite of not loving the shed, Nicolette let it remain. Happily, the inside is a far cry from the unsympathetic green exterior. The wood has been left unpainted, so all the knots show through. This makes a soothing backdrop, complementing Nicolette's colourful, semi-abstract landscapes created out of her love of nature and photography. She has added a few pieces of furniture, including a futon and an armchair, to relax in when not painting at her easel.

This shed was an uninspiring start to Nicolette's desire for a studio of her own. But another artist has since joined her, and with encouragement from her and other friends, she has turned a blind eye to its physical shortcomings and now is able to paint and enjoy the peace and calm within.

"Easily seduced, I begin to like the shed. I just have to repaint the outside to let it slip gently into the landscape and stop glaring at me."

opposite and inset In spite of its rather strident exterior, the shed, set in peaceful countryside, is a haven of calm and creativity inside.

above Dwarfed by an ancient ash tree, the black-painted clapboard shed sits at the end of a long, narrow garden.

left The panoramic windows offer an unparalleled view of the meadow beyond.

opposite The bright red door extends a warm welcome to visitors.

Aileen's Dad died some years ago and left her a small amount of money. She decided to spend it on a studio where she could do exactly as she pleased, and that included sitting doing nothing whenever she wasn't painting.

Graham, her partner, built the clapboard shed according to a dream that Aileen had about her Dad. It is set, fittingly, in the southwest corner of their pretty garden (yard), on the edge of the village of New Buckenham in Norfolk, England.

The house dates back to the Middle Ages and is part of a terrace. The shed is reached by walking up some steps and along a path to the end of the long and narrow garden. Neat and black, with a bright red door, it peers out of the shadow of an ancient ash tree, whose branches seem to arch down and protect it. The tree is one of the biggest in the village. Out across the peaceful meadow beyond, there are views of curving fields, other majestic trees, and, in the distance, a church tower.

The windows of the shed give Aileen a panoramic view of the meadow but they are all quite crude and do not open. She plans to replace a couple with double-glazing, which should help conserve heat in winter and keep the place cool in summer. The studio itself, jam-packed with easels and canvases, has been painted white, to add to the overall light and airy feel.

Aileen is forever grateful to her Dad and Graham for providing this shed and giving her the space where she can truly be herself.

"I had a dream some months after he died. We were walking together around a large estate carrying a delicate flowering plant, with its roots exposed. It seemed like a dowsing wand. We wondered where to plant it. Having reached a boundary to the southwest, we knew this was the place."

Kelly's spacious shed is called "Bow House Studio" after her house, which has a distinctive overhanging roof. Its location, on Rhode Island, couldn't be more idyllic, resting in a light-filled forest glade, down a winding gravel road, past a farm and river marshland.

The multi-functional studio is made up of an old barn and a lean-to, which was added in 2012. It has taken a lot of hard work to get thus far, and every year Kelly makes a few more improvements.

The barn had been a mechanic's shed, complete with old cars and equipment rusting inside, while the forest, an ever-shifting free spirit, was fast encroaching. Kelly and her lumberjack father had to decide whether to let the forest win or reclaim the land to create the extra studio space that Kelly needed. The decision made, her father cleared away some trees so they could get on with the renovation and modernization.

The serene setting is the perfect backdrop for creative work. Kelly shares her studio with others who come here to create their own art or to teach. Inside the barn, there are separate, informally divided areas for different themes and activities, from mixed media painting and sculpture to pastels and photography. Colorful paintings adorn the walls. There's even a little easel and painting materials for Kelly's daughter Ava.

far right A historic barn and a recently built lean-to have been converted into an enormous studio. The forest glade setting could not be more idyllic.

inset Kelly has a unique collection of hand-forged historic keys—inspiraton for future art.

"The cedar panels and high vaulted ceilings give my mind room to think big, and freely make art that is my signature style... a deconstruction of common structure with big color and bold shape."

opposite above Keys play an important and symbolic role in Kelly's art.

left High ceilings and plenty of natural light make the barn a wonderful working space for artists.

opposite below Various chisels are kept close to hand, hanging from a magnetic strip.

below Wooden cubbyholes are used for storage and to display quirky objects.

above right A tray of colored chalks, ready to be used by one of the artists who share the studio with Kelly.

The lean-to, a later addition to the studio, houses, among other things, Kelly's "Keys to the Cure" exhibition. Using an interplay of paint, encaustic, photography, and sculpture, this was established with the Regenerative Medicine Foundation and looks at the body's ability to heal itself and unlock the mysteries of life. Inside an antique cabinet of curiosities, Kelly safely stores various objects, such as hand-forged historic keys and locks dating back two hundred years, found objects, and written words to inspire. They are kept are on show until they come to life in her work.

Light streams in through the double doors and fanlight, the roof lights in the lean-to, and the windows all around, making the space a photographer's and artist's dream. Inspiration is everywhere, and, as one of Kelly's friends says, "It is a place to find yourself, a place to call a 'soulful artistic home.'"

"My approach is quite different... In the town studio I am working with scale, and the sculptures I make are large."

In a very large studio, all 3,200 square feet of it, in Fall River, Massachusetts, **Susan** has channeled her energies and talents into large and sculptural artworks—quite a departure from the small gouache artworks on paper that she produced when working from the dining room of her home. She calls that studio "Sailshade Studios," reflecting her use of sailcloth in installations and the stitched canvas paintings she creates. Susan describes some of her work as "fabric sculpture."

The shed shown here has cedar shingle cladding on the outside and bare wood inside. Fittingly, the space has a maritime air about it, with the exposed ceiling beams resembling the ribs of an upturned boat. It was originally built to house a 13-foot sailing canoe, with outriggers, belonging to Susan's writer husband, Alan, which he used for his forays onto the water to record birdsong for his book. When out of the water, the canoe is suspended from the ceiling of the shed with ropes and pulleys, suggesting further links with the sea and ponds of New England. Its deep blue painted hull makes a splash of vivid color against the brown of the wood and complements Susan's artworks lined up along one wall.

Susan works on the mezzanine floor, which has been created at one end, cordoned off with a wooden balustrade. A small built-in ladder leads to this cozy nook, where she paints. Underneath it, there is valuable storage space for boating equipment and other random items, covered over with a blue tarpaulin.

The rest of the space is a part-time gallery. Shelves have been worked into the sides of the shed for storing boat paraphernalia but they are also used for occasional displays of small artworks. Susan and Alan often travel to Europe, and she captures the landscapes of her visits. Several groups of these works were painted in Wales and Cleethorpes, on the northeast coast of England.

above The tall ceiling has made it possible to create a mezzanine floor at one end of the shed, and to hang a canoe on a pulley system from the bare beams.

inset From the driveway, it's hard to imagine how much space there is inside the shed.

left All the creature comforts are present in Sarah's shed, so she can sculpt and paint to her heart's content

right The grass roof makes the shed appear almost a part of the landscape, while its train-car shape links it with the railroad tracks at the end of the garden.

With railroad tracks running at the bottom of her garden (yard), **Sarah's** wooden shed, designed specifically in the shape of a small train car, suits its setting perfectly. It has a curved "living" grass roof, and when viewed from the house above, this patch of green can be seen as part of the surrounding landscape.

Sarah's shed was her gift to herself on her sixtieth birthday. However, it wasn't just the gift of a building but also of the space and time to be the artist she had always intended to be that came with it. For a long time, Sarah had promised herself that when she was "properly grown up," she would return to her art, which she had deserted for health and financial reasons for many years. To that end, she wanted a beautiful sculpted form in the garden, where she could paint, make a mess, or simply sit and do nothing. In short, a studio—somewhere warm, dry, and light, where she would not have to tidy away her paintings or clay busts and figures. More important, it is a place where she can truly be herself.

Reached by stone steps leading down from the house, the shed is set up with all the conveniences of running water, electricity, and a wood-burning stove, so Susan can remain here for most of the day, even in winter, if she chooses. The green roof is not only attractive, but it also helps to insulate the shed. Adjustable wooden shelving blends in with the paneled walls and is filled with boxes and baskets of the equipment that Sarah needs for her work.

"This shed is for me to bloom in and enjoy my autumn... It gives me permission and a place to do that chrysalis thing. I find it hard to give myself time to be in my shed. It will take a while to ease myself out of the 'oughts' and 'musts.'"

"When disaster struck and the world fell apart, the shed became a refuge, a precious sanctuary, safe from intrusions: 'entrance only by private invitation'!"

This is the last shed built by a master craftsman before he decided his back was no longer up to the task. It belongs to **Chris**, for whom it is not just a pretty wooden hut in her Norfolk garden (yard) but a second home, a haven, a studio, even a hide, from where she can watch all the toings and froings of nature, birds, and other wildlife. Often she will sit by a window either quietly reading or listening to music or birdsong.

The skill of the craftsman shows through in the shed's construction. It is beautifully designed and made. With its pale blue tongue-and-groove exterior and varying shades of white inside, it has something of a Scandinavian feel about it. There are windows on three sides, as well as a roof light and a glazed door. A clever design feature is the single shelves that run between the casement window and the pane of glass above it at each end of the shed.

Chris uses one end of the studio to paint in and the other for relaxation. The studio space contains a desk and an easel, on which Chris paints her watercolors, and samples of her finished work and work-in-progress decorate the wall. There are shelves and storage boxes for her art materials. The opposite end, meanwhile, is more like a comfortable sitting room, complete with a leather wing chair and throw and an oversized "thread-spool" coffee table. There are potted plants upon the chest of drawers, and a sheaf of dried lavender hanging from the ceiling. A floor-to-ceiling bookcase contains books and personal treasures.

When Chris feels the urge to paint or write, the shed is her creative space, exciting and enjoyable, but it is also her healing space, where she reflects on life and comes to terms with it.

opposite Beautifully designed and built, the shed has a Scandinavian feel about it.

above and inset Chris's shed has been divided into two distinct areas: one for painting, the other for relaxation.

Dora bought this American chestnut barn, to be her studio, entirely from the proceeds of her own painting sales. She and her husband Trip then had to have it transported the forty miles from North Attleboro to their home in Westport, Massachusetts.

Dora considers the time and trouble involved more than worth it. Her shed is an historic building: a late eighteenth-century "drive-through" dairy barn, with white cedar shingles on the walls and red cedar on the roof. If Dora had not bought it, the building would have been demolished as part of a land sale.

The original timber frame construction is modeled after comparable buildings of medieval Europe. In keeping with the theme, and inspired by a trip to thirteenth-century Salisbury Cathedral in England, Dora and her friend Tony Millham designed a 24-foot metalwork rail, to span the upper loft, which was built over one of the original three milking bays. Tony, a

top The single-story building alongside the barn is where Dora frames all her work. Rows of cork glued together make an unusual and original gallery backdrop.

above An old printer's tray has its compartments filled with shells and a tiny nest.

right In a space devoted to painting, work in progress doesn't have to be tidied away at the end of the day.

"real deal" blacksmith, then forged it. Reached by a white wooden staircase, the loft serves as an office and studio. Six skylights facing north give perfect, bright, diffused north light, making it ideal for painting in.

The space is entirely open-plan, with no dividing walls, but a large sixteenth-century carved doorway of English oak, and as hard as iron, frames the gap between two vertical posts as if there were a door. The arch does, however, indicate a degree of separation. Behind it, is a compact corner kitchen, complete with sink, stove, and refrigerator.

Taking center stage are Dora's three easels, and hanging on the surrounding walls, and propped up against them, are some of her paintings. A wonderful piece of wall art is a circle of old paintbrushes, while a glass cabinet holds an intriguing collection of objects that Dora has collected on her travels around the world, such as Kenyan bead works and pieces of pottery. The wood-burning stove nearby, together with the central heating, provide all the warmth that the enormous space needs in winter.

The single-story "Frame Shop" alongside has a cathedral ceiling with three skylights, making it as light and airy as the main studio. This is where Dora frames all her work. Stretched along one wall is a board made entirely out of collected corks, making an ingenious backdrop for drawings and paintings. And then there is the chicken shed...

above This necklace, collected on one of Dora's many trips abroad, is made out of broken clay pipe stems.

below Even the chicken shed is well designed.

"My studio is a very happy, light-filled space for me. I have room for supplies and books, great views of the landscape, and easy access for visitors... It is the center of my daily life, but removed from household activities."

above The studio is attached to Johanna's home and can be reached through the master bedroom. With cedar shingles and identical windows, it looks like a mini version of the house.

After years of making do with part of the garage as her studio, which was incredibly cold in winter, then a spare second-floor bedroom, **Johanna** built her specially tailored workspace. She enlisted the help of a local Rhode Island architect, who had designed the studios of artists that she knew.

There were a couple of constraints that had to be addressed at the outset. Johanna wanted the studio to be attached to her house and the architecture of both to be consistent. She also wanted there to be an entrance from the driveway. To meet zoning and setback requirements, the only option was to attach it to the master bedroom.

Johanna's architect was very understanding of her needs. He took into account that she is right-handed and positioned everything in the studio accordingly so that she could work in the most efficient way. The space is divided informally into three: a corner for painting, a table for encaustics, and a bench for framing.

The studio is very much a workspace of simple finishes and functional design. The cathedral ceiling makes it very light and airy, and there are glass doors on both sides and north-facing skylights, to give Joanna as much natural light as possible. Displayed paintings are spotlighted by track lighting, while task lights are to hand on dull days.

Much of the wall space is taken up with Johanna's work, which is mainly watercolors. Dotted around there are also some clay pieces from the time when she swapped paints for a potter's wheel.

above Everything in the studio has been specially designed to suit Johanna and her way of working, with the space divided informally into three: for painting, making encaustics, and framing.

right Johanna painted this pair of Timberland boots for a charity project. They stand on display on an open shelf above her table.

It's hard to believe that Gill's spacious and light-filled shed was once a garage, complete with a kennel. Unusually, it was this south-facing building that made her decide to buy the house, which is off the beaten track but fairly close to the town of Diss in Norfolk, England. The shed is hardly visible from the house and to reach it, Gill first had to walk through her semi-wild garden (yard) of blackberries, willows, and various shrubs, through a gate, across a vegetable patch, then through another gate.

Gill rebuilt the garage following her own design, to make the space a home from home and give her the maximum amount of natural light and comfort. She added the biggest Velux windows she could find, insulated everywhere, and installed under-floor heating. She also included a sofa bed, and a piano. All she needed was the murmur of the radio before settling down to sculpt, write, or paint.

Folding doors allowed the space to be intimate or wide open. And whenever she wanted to take a break, she sat on the African-inspired

"Maybe the shed was too comfortable, maybe too smart for a painter to mess around in. The next studio is ready to use and I won't be at all precious about keeping the floor clean."

veranda, watching and listening to swifts reeling overhead in the summer, a cuckoo calling softly in spring, and owls hooting in the darkness.

After all this work, though, Gill wondered whether the space wasn't practical enough. Perhaps a less beautiful but more practical shed would suit her needs better...

Gill has since moved to Suffolk. Not as pretty and definitely much smaller, this old flint and brick building was once used to store coal but it is more or less ready for Gill to move in and start painting, drawing, and making. She intends to paint the walls white, to make the best of the light from the single Velux window, but practically everything she needs is already in place, from charcoal and paint to all sorts of canvases, wire, and pastels, as well as a small wood-burning stove in the corner, to keep her warm in winter. Gill is looking forward to taking up residence, where she knows she won't mind the spills and splashes on the paneled and flint walls or on the wooden floor.

above left The tall ceiling and many windows allowed the light to blast through, making the perfect space for painting. The soft green tongue-and-groove walls provided a pleasing neutral backdrop for the display of artworks.

above right Although it is not nearly as smart as her previous studio, this flint and brick building in the garden of her new home suits Gill better, in spite of being much smaller.

Chapter 2

Sheds **for living**

In these difficult economic times, buying a conventional house, upsizing, or even holding on to a house can be a challenge for many people. But if they have the resources and imagination, a shed can be a creative way of leading a different, less encumbered life, and a cost-effective way of making their homes work for them. Planning consent may be needed, but not always. Then the imagination is set free!

Such sheds can meet a desire for simplicity, a need to be to be away from the complexity and hustle of contemporary life. When these small sheds are homes, the space must be used efficiently, simply, and therefore beautifully. They may even contain a bed as somewhere to retreat to and dream and share—or not.

The shed can also take care of the stuff of living—sports equipment, inflatable swimming pool, oars, games, family belongings—things that you want to keep but have nowhere else to store them. It's also somewhere to put those things that you're not ready to part with just yet or that might come in useful one day...

We may also need to store gardening stuff—the allotment (see page 120), farm or garden shed is the place for the tools, seeds and other paraphernalia that make it all possible.

Sometimes, sheds are retreats with chairs and tables, a stove and a kettle. On a rainy day what can be better than brewing coffee or tea and gazing out at the fruits of our labour or just into space?

"It's got a lovely light and feel to it in the early mornings and late afternoons, very relaxing and peaceful. It's quiet, warm, and cozy, especially at night with my candles lit, listening to the rain and wind outside..."

Hidden behind a trellis in the garden (yard) of a Buddhist community house, in Glastonbury, England, a humble shed has been turned into a luxurious gem. **Jeanette** has used layer upon layer of fabric, on the furniture, walls, and ceiling, as well as carefully chosen pictures and objects, to create her very personal and private retreat.

At the far end of the shed, the bed, with its multicolored and textured silk cushions and fabric canopy, creates an opulent feel. Her desk, at the other end, by sliding glass doors, is bathed in natural light, making the perfect spot for writing. In the summer, with the door open, she can feel the breeze as she works; in the winter, she can look through the trellis unseen at the birds feeding in the garden.

Although there is no kitchen or bathroom, the shed seems like a home in miniature, full of Jeanette's treasured possessions. There are framed pictures decorating the walls, photographs of loved ones propped up on shelves, and a noticeboard by her desk covered with postcards from friends. Plants make the space almost as lush as the garden—they stand in terra-cotta pots on the floor, in a hanging basket, and on every available surface—and lilies in a vase fill the air with their heady scent.

above Flowers in vases and plants in pots help turn a humble shed into a cozy retreat.

left Covered with cushions in sumptuous fabrics, the canopied bed stretches luxuriously from wall to wall.

opposite above A wooden trellis helps provide privacy, especially in summer, when it's covered in scented climbers.

opposite below The shed has been filled with personal treasures and mementoes, making it a very personal space.

"As you can see there are two sheds, just in case it gets a bit lonely and I need a friend to come and spend some proper time..."

Standing side by side among a number of sheds in her Norfolk garden (yard) (see also pages 184-5) are **Lizzy's** living van and accompanying shed, now a spare bedroom.

Both structures have intriguing histories. Although there are similarities, the van is not a gypsy wagon but a working van that plowmen used to sleep in when not operating their gyrotillers. These huge rotating plows on iron wheels were used around the clock in Britain during World War II to break new ground—at that time, food was scarce and every possible step was taken to increase production. Meanwhile, the shed is a recycled sauna that once belonged to Lizzy's mother.

Resting on its hefty iron wheels, the van is reached by a wooden staircase to the veranda, which Lizzy built. Painted the same brilliant blue, with sunshine yellow around the windows, the van and shed share the veranda. This looks out over the fields toward the setting sun. All year around there are spectacular sunsets when the veranda is bathed in soft pinks, oranges, and reds.

Now a guest room and a retreat, the van is much as it was seventy-odd years ago. Although renovated and brightened up with primary colors, it still retains most of its original features, adding to its charm. Inside, then as now, is a built-in bunk bed, now turned into a double, hooks for hammocks, a wood-burning stove, and cupboards.

A lovely decorative touch is the stained glass window, which the previous owner put in. This, together with the glass skylight, known as a "mollycroft" on traveling vans, increases the amount of natural light.

The "sauna" shed has been given a corrugated tin roof, its curved shape echoing that of the van. To fill in the space between the original structure and the roof, a panel was inserted and a friend painted a picture of a horse and Lizzy's old cat, Margot, sitting on the fence.

Painted the same bright blue inside and out as the van, this is a basic but cozy retreat, where Lizzy has created another built-in bed. She has also put up shelves and introduced an old-fashioned metal washbasin and a pitcher (jug) stand.

opposite and above Libby's living van, and the converted sauna next door are both guest bedrooms in the garden of her home. Painted the same striking blue and yellow inside and out, they are a reflection of Lizzy's ingenuity.

left The living van contained a bunk bed originally, when it was used by a couple of itinerant plowmen. Libby has since turned it into a double, making the most of the available space.

above All that's needed to heat up water for tea and coffee, and warm up the hut on chilly days, is the wood-burning stove.

opposite above and inset The inside of the hut is very cozy, with drapes at the windows and a beautiful handmade quilt on the bed. Although tiny, the kitchen is surprisingly well equipped.

overleaf Jen's refuge is one in a line of mismatching black beach huts, where all the owners know one another and enjoy sharing the salty air.

Hidden behind sand dunes, this friendly community of black wooden beach huts faces the North Sea, on the outskirts of the Suffolk village of Walberswick. In summer, and for a few glorious months, their owners open their doors and windows, and tea kettles are put on stoves to boil water for tea or coffee. Cakes and cookies appear on small tables outside to share with beach hut neighbors and daytrippers.

The village has all the amenities that the beach hut owners could need, including a smattering of pubs, a small food store, and public toilets. There's also a rowing boat ferry that takes them to buy freshly caught fish from the local fishmonger on the river estuary. This is living at its simplest.

Jen has had her beach hut for about 28 years. She has decked it out exactly to suit herself, with everything she could need for passing the time of day at peace by the sea. She's made simple blue-and-white checked curtains for the windows and for covering the underneath of the worktop. There's a small wood-burning stove to sit around when it's cold and damp. From the bed, with its vintage quilt, she can gaze out over the fields to the dunes.

The hut is filled with beach treasures and curios. Around the stove is a collection of stones with holes in them. According to folklore, these fairy stones ward off evil spirits and protect fishermen, and it's believed that they even help sleep. Simple hooks in the walls and ceilings are useful storage for the paraphernalia of living. Even the back of the stable door is put to good use, storing frying pans, mugs, and a hot-water bottle.

For Jen, her hut is her refuge. Although quite basic, it is domestic and comfortable, and she can fully experience the elements, the seasons, and the roar of the sea. Such is the sea's power that one year the tide came in so high that a number of sheds were shifted several feet. And every year, like her neighbors, Jen has to give her hut a new coat of black tar varnish to protect it from the wind and salty air.

"I realize my hut is a sort of grown-up doll's house where I can express another part of myself—the part that never grew up."

above left Sue's desk stretches along almost the entire length of one wall in the room that once housed the village store. Sue does her sketching at the section of desk shown here.

above center The one-story lean-to, squeezed in between two neighboring properties, has been transformed into a compact and characterful home.

above right All the furniture in The Hovel has been made by local craftspeople, which gives the space a sense of unity. Baskets that Sue has made hang from a ladder sandwiched between two walls.

Sue's one-story, shed-like house is a lean-to in the middle of her Suffolk village. Her affectionate name for it is The Hovel, after the traditional peasant practice of creating dwellings that leaned against other buildings.

It's not known when The Hovel was squeezed in between the two neighboring properties but, over the years, it has been chopped up, patched up, and changed so that it's a real mishmash of materials, from flint and clay lump brick to shiplap boarding. It has seen many different uses, too—as a workplace, store, and garage for the local grocer's delivery van. Before she moved here to live after retiring, Sue used it as her basket-making studio. As and when she could afford to, she made little improvements so that eventually it became comfortable enough to live in.

Inside, Sue has created a compact and perfect home. Traces of its previous role as her studio are still in evidence, with basket weave plant holders, containers, and platters decorating the space.

A stable door at the front opens immediately onto a living/working room. Drawing the eye immediately upward are some of Sue's beautiful handmade baskets hanging from hooks

"As there is no garden with The Hovel, I have an allotment. The allotment shed is my 'other place' and I have much joy just fiddling about, making woodpiles... sitting, thinking... Sometimes I even garden!"

along a ladder sandwiched between two walls. The large storefront windows and the roof light make this room, and the living room immediately behind, light and airy. With space at such a premium, there are no internal doors, and the living room is separated by a curtain from a very small sleeping cupboard, just big enough for Sue's bed. At the back of the house is a small shower and bathroom. Needless to say, all that's needed to heat Sue's home is a small, wood-burning stove.

All of Sue's domestic needs are more than adequately met by The Hovel, except for one thing—she doesn't have a garden (yard). To put that right, she has an allotment (see page 120 for explanation) outside the village, complete with a shed. Home to all the usual gardening tools, it's also where Sue keeps a wonderful, high-backed wicker chair for sitting in the shed and having a cup of tea, brewed on the small gas stove.

Tucked in among various shrubs at the bottom of **Chris's** garden (yard) is her Romanian shepherd's hut, painted in muted greens to blend in with the landscape. It is set in its own little valley—deliciously romantic—protected by the land that curls around it. Close by is Glastonbury Tor, considered to be one of England's most well-known spiritual sites.

There is fittingly a spiritual and aesthetic purpose to the shepherd's hut. Everything about it supports the peace that Chris seeks, and she starts each day here, meditating and reflecting before meeting the world.

In summer, Chris often sleeps in the hut, where she feels more attuned to the "cycles of the moon, the sense of the earth beneath and the sky above..." and protected from the magnetic fields caused by cell phone masts, to which she has developed a sensitivity. The bed can be curtained off, and the drapes and bedding are all soft, gentle hues, in keeping with the tranquillity and peace of the surroundings. Chris tells of how, when she throws open the windows in the morning, all she can hear are the singing birds, rustling trees, and the splashing of the Lambrook, a small stream that runs alongside.

Paraffin lamps hang from the ceiling, which has been left in its natural state, while the walls are painted a soft white. Additional atmospheric lighting is provided by the pretty brass candleholders, mounted on the wall above an old pine church pew.

above Chris often sleeps in the shepherd's hut because of the sense of peace it brings her, with Glastonbury Tor close by.

opposite above When closed, the drapes at the windows and around the bed create a cocoon-like retreat.

opposite below Away from the distractions of home, the hut is the perfect place for Chris to meditate every morning.

"This is a place to fully appreciate the profound beauty of the natural world... It provides a space to listen deeply inside to the promptings of my soul and to daydream without interruption."

Mel has now moved on from this house and shed in Norfolk, England. The shed was her refuge as she came to terms with the loss of her daughter, Rosie.

The house was full of young lodgers, and Mel enjoyed their comings and goings, and hearing about their lives in her warm, welcoming kitchen, but there were times when she needed to be alone with her own life and memories. A friend built the shed using recycled windows and doors. This small outside space overlooked the garden and in it Mel contemplated and remembered, gazing at objects and drawings that connected her to memories of love and loss. No reading or writing took place. There was no radio or computer. The shed was a place of quiet and healing, bringing together the past, the present, and the future.

The garden pressed up against the window panes and waved about in, what Mel describes as, "an underwater sort of way." The shed was relaxed in its boundaries between outside and inside. Spiders and beetles, flies and bees bumble and buzzed in and out. Leaves blew in, and little stones gathered under the door. There was beauty here, mixed in with all the sadness, with the unpainted plywood walls, the garden looking in, and the clay horse on the window sill. And there was also healing, as Mel explains:

"There is some god too, so the bruised shocks from outside meet this shed air and are slowly transformed and made calm. There were no words to tangle the space... And the minutes and months and four years pass. Things die—ladybugs, spiders, tears, and bees. Things live—ladybugs, spiders, bees, and tears. Time passes, time passes, and winter whoops into spring... Love arrived, thick and unnoticed, in the first frenzy. There is love from Rosie, my daughter, who said, 'Here, Mum, this is a place we can be.'"

And I am alone too. Breathing a bruised and shocked world together with a quiet shed world into something different where words like sacred, agony, flower and bee fuse and lay at our feet—a way forward!'

above The peace and quiet provided by the sparsely furnished shed helped Mel to come to terms with her loss. She could sit in the comfy chair by the window, deep in thought.

opposite Built in the shadow of the house, the lean-to wooden shed was a peaceful haven in a busy world. Grasses, shrubs, and flowers surrounded it, adding to the tranquillity.

"It gets a spring clean most years and is re-felted often so it's dry and a good storage space, not just for stuff but also for memories and stories."

Bryn has built a beautiful eco-house on the side of a hill in her village near the Suffolk coast, to accompany her new shed and this mellowing ledge-type wagon. It must be at least seventy or eighty years old and was almost certainly a horse-drawn wagon in its heyday. Now missing its wheels and propped up on chopped-off telegraph poles, the wagon has certainly seen better days. Its paintwork has been softened by the wind, sun, and rain, and ivy has taken a firm hold on the weather-worn wood. Cats shelter underneath in dens of discarded bricks and tiles.

Bryn has had her wagon since the 1980s. When she spied it through some undergrowth, she fell in love with it. It had been lived in by a local man, a barber, but was now empty, except for a mouse nest in one of the cupboards. Bryn was all too pleased to buy it for £40 and have it transported to her garden (yard) as a playroom for her nine-year-old daughter.

The wagon has had a few different uses since then. One year she camped out at the top of her garden and used it as a kitchen, while guests, who wanted to spend their vacation by the sea, took up residence in her house. At another time, her daughter decided to "leave home" and moved in.

Today, the caravan houses some of her bee equipment. When we visited, there was an impenetrable wall of jars and boxes that made it almost impossible to get inside! However, our visit did prompt a long overdue clear out, which uncovered the bed and cupboards from the time when the wagon was lived in.

above In spite of its rundown appearance, the old wagon still exudes a considerable charm and is an important presence in Bryn's life.

opposite With its peeling and faded paint and probing ivy taking a firm hold, the wagon looks like it has always belonged in this setting.

Rachel's garden shed is tiny, although that in itself would be difficult to prove, as it is camouflaged almost entirely by an abundance of bamboo, lavender, twisted hazel, sundry small shrubs, and a lovely pink scented climbing jasmine. Together, they have almost succeeded in making the shed disappear completely. All that's visible is the aqua-painted door.

Mother Nature certainly has the upper hand with the shed, and Rachel has left her to it. She enjoys retreating here after her commute from the city of Norwich, in Norfolk, England, to relax in among the greenery, away from the house. Cushions and blankets are kept inside the shed for such occasions, easily pulled out either for lying on and looking at the sky or for picnics.

For such a small shed, there are a remarkable number of things stored inside, and most of them serve to connect Rachel to the great outdoors. She keeps boats and sailing paraphernalia for river adventures, a tent and camping equipment for vacations in the wild, and beach sundries for day-trips to the seaside. There are also cushions and blankets to put down in the garden.

right Nature has taken a firm but welcome hold on Rachel's shed, which is almost completely covered with greenery .

"It's a tiny shed but perfect for me! I can sit outside in this tranquil space created by the shrubs and climbers; relax in the shade with a book or in the evening with a glass of wine, catching the last of the day's sun as it sets in the west."

Caroline's wish to live where she chose, and as she chose, is a fraught, yet hugely inspiring tale. She battled local planners, as well as other residents, to get to live in this unique building.

Neither overlooked nor overlooking anyone else, the shed is situated among the gentle rolling Somerset hills in England's West Country, surrounded by woods and fields. From the outside, it appears nothing out of the ordinary, apart from one wall that Caroline has created out of logs of varying sizes, with a band of glass bottles, 544, to be precise, in the middle. Set in a double row, the bottles create a wall two feet thick. Of various shapes, sizes, and colors, the bottles provide excellent insulation, as well as letting in a beautiful greenish mottled light to the living area.

Caroline is living a small carbon-footprint life, off-grid with the resources she has around her. Solar panels, a small wind turbine, a wood-burning stove, and a small hydro-system and waterwheel, powered by the small stream running alongside her land, provide all her energy needs. There is no mains electricity and if, for some reason, she doesn't have enough power stored, there are lanterns and candles, followed by an early night.

There is nothing new in Caroline's shed at all. The mismatching windows and the kitchen units come from other people's houses and are patchworked together. Even the shelves recycled from her grandson's bedroom still have his felt-tip drawings on the side. The walls are untreated oriented strand board (OSB), an engineered wood particleboard, inexpensive and relatively environmentally friendly. Normally, the material is used for construction and covered with plasterboard but Caroline has chosen to leave it exposed. All the furniture is secondhand, too, and that's exactly the way Caroline likes it.

above As part of her wish to lead a small carbon-footprint life, Caroline has created a small hydro-system and water wheel by the nearby stream, to provide some of her energy needs.

opposite and inset The end wall of this chalet-like shed sets it apart from others. Made out of cut logs lined up on their sides, with a band of various recycled bottles in the center, the wall is practical as well as decorative, providing extra insulation.

Brenda's little wooden shed was originally built as part of her greenhouse project, to act as a potting shed, but it quickly took on a life of its own—there are no pots and only a small vegetable garden remains. It has, however, become her place of escape, should she need one, from running the busy Paquachuck Inn on Westport Point in Massachusetts. Standing right on the harbor's edge in the hotel grounds, the shed is the ideal place to take in a deep breath and gather one's thoughts.

Behind its green doors, this simple and rustic shed is a hideaway, which also provides sleeping accommodation for visiting friends, family, and their children. Squeezed into one corner, designated as the bedroom, is a bunk bed. Although comfortable, there is nothing precious about the interior—the drapes hang from makeshift rails, and the furniture has seen better days—which makes it an idea play space as well for children of any age.

For anyone who braves the water at one of the nearby beaches, there is an outside shower by the door, with its roof open to the elements. Brenda had the shower built fairly recently and incorporated a rather lovely recycled window. The new wood will, eventually, weather to the soft gray of the shed.

above Inside, the shed provides unfussy sleeping accommodation for Brenda's friends. Although nothing matches, the haphazardness is enjoyable.

opposite and inset In spite of their obvious differences, the rather grand greenhouse and the humble wooden shed complement each other. The wood of the roofless outdoor shower will, in time, fade to the same mellow gray as the shed.

The shed's stately companion is a Lord & Burnham greenhouse, almost one hundred years old. Made of cypress and cast iron, it belonged to Brenda's father. She had it moved here as a reminder of her childhood but it is also an oasis. On a part of the coast where the elements are often extreme—hurricanes do come this way—the greenhouse can be relied upon to provide life and light throughout the year.

Raised on a rough stone wall, the metal greenhouse, with its flagstone floors, is an otherworldly space where Brenda entertains friends. Although it has the character of age, with peeling paint and rusty metal, it still has an air of grandeur, and is a magnificent backdrop to Brenda's humble shed. At night, lit up by a glitter ball, it is a romantic setting, surrounded by ferns and palms.

The greenhouse, which is almost one hundred years old, is somewhat grand compared to Brenda's shed. At night, it becomes an enchanting space to be shared with friends, lit only by candles and reflections from the glitter ball.

Meredith's shed, on the far left of its companions, stands in the grounds of her home, a condominium in a seventeenth-century house. Over the years, her living space has been downsized, and the shed plays an important role in looking after things she has no room for but can't bear to part with—at least for the time being.

Ipswich, Massachusetts, has the distinction of having the most seventeenth- and eighteenth-century houses still in existence in the United States. The Sherborne-Wilson House, built in 1685, is one such building. No longer a family home, it was converted into five condominiums in 1986, and **Meredith** moved into one of them.

Meredith had been downsizing for years. Before she moved to the condo, she had lived in a fifteen-room farmhouse, a twelve-room Victorian cottage, and, finally, an eight-room house with an attic and a basement. In spite of reducing her belongings drastically with each move, she still had too much for her new home. Ever practical, she bought a small shed, purely and simply for storage, and had it assembled in the parking area behind the house, next to a row of other condo sheds.

She put up tall steel shelves on two walls, and her bicycle hangs from a third. The small space filled up in no time. A great lover of the outdoors, Meredith stores her camping gear and gardening equipment here, as well as out-of-season clothes. But she also uses the shed as a holding pen, storing all those things she no longer needs or uses but to which she still has an emotional attachment and is not quite ready to give up.

"When I bought a three-room condominium in the historic Sherborne-Wilson House... I had hard choices to make. Everything had to be carefully evaluated and what I could bear to part with was given away or sold. I find that it's actually easier to get rid of things after they've been out of sight in my shed for a few months or years."

"I'm so excited to have a space of my own, where I can draw, meditate, read, and relax. I will be able to sit on the steps, contemplating the view and sometimes even spend the night there, listening to the night sounds."

Gail got lucky. She discovered this old shepherd's hut in the meadow belonging to a family friend. Left to rot long ago by previous owners, it had sunk deep into sand by the river on the property and been squashed by the overhanging bough of a willow.

To recover the hut, she and her husband Pete had to dig it out of the sand and clear away years' worth of debris. They found newspapers between the two "skins" of wood that were one hundred years old to the month! They even removed some planks of timber from the walls to make the job easier (these are now stored under the shed until renovation starts).

Once Gail's brother Andrew helped free the hut from the willow with a chainsaw, they wrapped straps around it, and a teleporter (telescopic lifting machine) was used to lift it high onto a trailer. They watched with trepidation but the seemingly fragile structure held out.

The hut is now sitting in the orchard at Gail's home near Diss, in Norfolk, England. It looks a little forlorn and very dilapidated but Gail loves it, with its huge, iron wheels and its sense of history. She plans to restore it, with a little help, and furnish it simply, including installing a wood-burning stove, which the hut would have had originally. She's even considering making a stained glass window for it.

above left and right As part of her restoration plans for the hut, Gail plans to supplement the tiny porthole window and circle of ventilation holes with windows, possibly a stained-glass one.

opposite and inset At least one hundred years old, this humble shepherd's hut has not aged gracefully but has somehow managed to hold on to its original iron wheels.

"Retirement planning: how to fill my time? Unimaginable. I have a compelling need for my own space, while not cutting myself off completely!"

Although **Helen** dreams of the past, this is a shed of the future, of what comes next in her life. Set at an angle in the corner of her large garden (yard) near Diss, in Norfolk, England, the shed looks out over the valley and fields beyond. Light streams in through the double French doors, which can be thrown wide open to nature. A tiny veranda facing south allows her to sit outdoors and follow the sun as it arcs across the sky. Friends often join her, perhaps saluting the sunset with a gin and tonic.

Custom-made to Helen's requirements, the shed has room for a sofa bed for sleeping out on warm summer nights and waking to the dawn chorus from the surrounding trees. The paintings are the ones she likes. It is simple, white and only has a few books. It has a wooden floor, is insulated throughout and is double-glazed for warmth in the winter. More important, there's also space for Helen's piano, and because the shed is so far from the house, she can play it, and also the flute, uninterrupted and without fear of disturbing others.

This gray-blue shed is not just for making music, however. There is a desk for writing, and it's also where Helen dreams and conjures up new possibilities and directions for her life.

left Facing south, the shed is a light-filled space, and the tiny veranda is a wonderful spot for enjoying the sunshine.

inset Making music is Helen's passion, and her shed, fitted with double-glazed windows, provides the perfect location away from the house where no one can hear her.

Although it is nowhere near the sea, **Paddy's** shed is, paradoxically, called the Boat House because her friend Cee (see pages 98–9) thought that the wooden stilts on which it stands made it look like one. Cee, the original owner, had designed the shed with a local architect but then moved to the coast, and Paddy took her place.

Of the four sheds that Paddy has in her luscious cottage garden, this is the first one a visitor will see on arriving at her Suffolk home. The clapboard paneling has been painted a soft gray, which makes a soothing contrast with the rust-red window frames and the subtle patina of the old roof pantiles. The shed is used primarily for storage, having been taken over by a mixture of home improvement tools and assorted paraphernalia so, for the present, there is no space for living.

The shed has an asymmetrical corrugated tin roof that extends out to cover the wood store. A secluded and sheltered veranda, with a bed and chairs, is surrounded by pretty flowers in pots and shrubs. This is a special retreat, both for time spent alone relaxing or socializing with a few close friends.

The bird boxes on the side of the shed are alive with chicks in the spring, and bird feeders, hanging from the nearby pergola, encourage frantic activity all year around.

As time goes by, Paddy reflects more and more about how and where she lives. She even wonders whether she could live in the shed. However, before that could happen, she has the difficult task of sorting through the precious things she is caretaking for dear departed friends. Once she has done that, the Boat House could, indeed, become her home.

above A wooden pergola entwined with grapevines provides welcome shade for the dining area just outside the shed.

opposite Paddy's charming shed looks completely at home in her cottage garden.

overleaf The shed's veranda is decked out with chairs and a bed, making it a favorite spot for relaxation.

"I built a nest box on the side wall, and every year I watch the great tits flying in and out and the babies fledge."

Chapter 3

Sheds **for makers**

Categorizing people and their sheds is problematic. It's a retreat, it's a studio, and it's an inheritance. Similarly, in the world of the "creative," there are categories and meanings about who is a maker, a craftsperson, a sculptor, a painter.

I asked a woman sculptor if she was a sculptor or a maker of things. She is a sculptor, she explained, on a journey of discovery rather than "for a market." Her work, being figurative, has been challenged. She has been told it is not "art"! When is an artist an artist; a sculptor a sculptor; a maker a maker, and a craftsperson a craftsperson? Does it matter? Possibly it matters to the women themselves. It is how they define themselves.

Everywhere, and for all time, there has been a human imperative to make beautiful objects. Objects dedicated to gods and goddesses, decoration on everyday utensils, shamanic depiction, and reflections of external and internal worlds. Imagination realized by creative hands brings pleasure and reassurance to all of us.

Some makers engage with their craft for their living— there is a primary financial imperative. For others, it is a journey of exploration and, for a lucky few, who are successful or can afford it, the creative urge means that they must and do make stuff.

In an industrialized world full of techno-wizardry, a return to the slow, the handmade, and a perfect imperfection provides soul, and reminds us of our individuality and beauty.

Jane's shed is on her allotment (see page 120 for explanation), which is just outside a village in Cambridgeshire, England where she lives. Although the shed she chose was "readymade," she was able to say where she wanted the doors: a single at one end and big double doors on the side, which open out onto glorious views over the surrounding fields. Jane is a textile and environmental artist, and the mellow green paint treatment and hanging woven work both inside and out have turned the shed from the ordinary into the creative.

It was fifteen years ago that Jane put up her shed and began to spend more time on the allotment. She started to grow willow, as well as vegetables, and the shed became her studio. The seasons were an intrinsic part of her creativity, as was passing the time of day with her fellow allotment holders.

She worked hard, too hard, and it took a bout of pneumonia in 2007 to prompt her to take stock and slow down. The shed then became an important part of her recovery. She would spend many a day there, taking in the pace of life in the allotments around her and re-evaluating her own life.

Jane still weaves, spins, and stitches, and communicates as an artist through "slow making," where the processes are deliberately slowed down. Her

above and inset Jane's readymade shed is her studio, adapted to include large double doors. Hazel and willow branches are stored in the smaller shed.

above right The day is spent juggling time between crafting and tending the allotment.

> "When recovering from pneumonia I was forced to stop the frantic activity that had become habit."

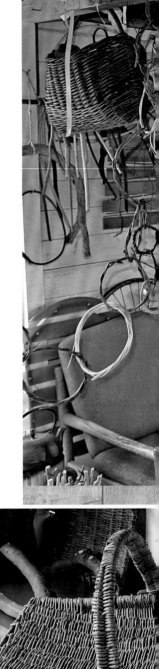

above With no electricity in the shed, the bucket stove provides the heating and also boils water for pots of tea.

above right Willow wreaths made by children as part of a project Jane worked on hang from the rafters.

below right One of the exquisite trugs that Jane has made out of willow.

far right Hazel and willow are entwined together to create unique sculptures, such as this duck.

shed is a testament to her creativity—an inspirational assortment of curls and spirals, baskets, trugs, and sculptures made of willow and hazel. Hanging from the rafters are willow wreaths, like Christmas garlands. The neat row of spades and forks at the back of the shed is a reminder that Jane is still a keen grower of vegetables, salads, and, of course, willow.

Taking well-earned breaks from her crafting and gardening, Jane will brew a pot of tea on the bucket stove by the door, which is also used to heat the shed—there is no electricity. Willow and other wood offcuts from her crafting are used to keep the stove going.

A smaller shed at the other end of her allotment is where Jane stores branches of hazel and willow, some of them propped up against the open-sided structure in fine weather, to dry out. Behind it is a row of beehives alive with activity, with the bees helping to pollinate all the allotment plants.

> "I just like sitting here, looking out at the garden or at things I am making, listening to radio plays and music, rain, and birds on the tin roof, mice in the walls."

This old building, situated on the edge of a Suffolk tidal bay on the English east coast, has had an interesting and checkered past. Originally an adjunct to an old brick farmhouse in the "middle of nowhere," it is now **Meg's** shed—completely functional, to suit her needs as a puppeteer, but in the most idyllic surroundings.

It seems strange to think now that it started life in the late nineteenth century as a pigpen, but signs of these humble origins remain—there are brick arches in the wall through which the pigs used to run in and out.

After the farm was sold, to be a guesthouse, complete with stables, the shed became a tack room. There are signs of this previous life, too, with the racks for hanging bridles, and a penciled list of the names and dates of the foals born here. After World War II it became a potting shed and general storeroom, but the end room ended up in the seventies as the rehearsal room of Hank Wangford, the country and western musician. So the artistic connections began.

Meg has worked in her shed since the eighties. Long and narrow, it is divided into four rooms, each performing its particular role in the running of Meg's puppetry company. The biggest room is the main studio, the creative hub. Here, Meg makes the puppets and devises her shows. There's a desk, often piled high with papers and materials, where she makes the puppets and draws storyboards and designs. In the plan chest close by, she

above A humble pigpen in the late nineteenth century, Meg's shed is now used for her puppetry business.

opposite The desk in the main studio, where Meg makes her puppets and devises her shows, is always piled high with papers, tools, and materials. Viewed through the window straight ahead, the wild garden outside is a soothing antidote to the breakneck creativity.

keeps her supplies of paper and card, as well as her most treasured drawings. An important piece of equipment, her sewing machine, lives in this room, too, on a separate small table. When time is running out to be ready for a new show, the space sometimes becomes a general workshop, with up to four people jammed in at one time.

Drawings, photographs, and postcards pepper the walls. There are pieces of artwork by her friends, together with a series of photographs of five generations of the female line of her family. This is her favorite room, with its views over the marsh. She makes sure she enjoys them, too, taking time out from making the puppets and their costumes whenever she can to relax.

Two further rooms are used for storage, where mountains of trunks, suitcases, and boxes are filled with the stars of previous puppet shows. The final room is Meg's small and tidy office with space for a desk and computer, where, she muses, she spends far too much time.

Tucked away in the field next door is a beautiful old showman's wagon.

"At times there are terrifying lists of what still has to be made by a deadline for a show. The books are all references for my artistic work about wildlife, puppets, theater, art, anatomy, and dance. There are boxes of tools and cloth, art materials, glues, tapes, nails, and screws."

left and inset There's scarcely a bare surface to be found in the studio. Even the walls are virtually covered over with family photographs, postcards, and artworks made by friends.

right An old traveling showman's wagon in the field next door is a mysterious presence.

At the end of a long bumpy lane near the source of the River Waveney, in Norfolk, England, is **Kathy's** home. On the other side of the lane, there is a vegetable plot and Kathy's workshop. It has its own little fenced garden (yard), with a table and chairs and views of the fen and the woods.

On cold, rainy days Kathy loves to snuggle up here with her dogs and cat and lose herself in work. She is a mixed media artist, specializing in wedding cake decoration, particularly freestanding figures, reminiscent of Giacometti sculptures. These elongated figures, often inspired by old movies, fairy tales, and high fashion, are both delicate and expressive.

Kathy thinks of herself as being like a hobbit in her little shed. She knows where everything is, and there's a place for everything, even though, as she fears, it probably looks an untidy mess to any visitor. On warm, sunny days she sits on the step just outside the wide French doors and feels a great sense of being a part of nature. The view can be quite a distraction, with the wonderful array of wildlife just beyond her window.

There was a time when it seemed that Kathy would have to move house. The thought of leaving her shed, her "best mate," behind filled her with more dread than leaving her home. Fortunately, her circumstances changed for the better and artist and shed remain very much a team.

left Shelves concealed by simple drapes and wicker baskets help Kathy keep some of her materials under wraps.

opposite above In fine weather, the doors are flung open.

opposite below Kathy's mixed media wedding cake decorations are graceful and delicate figures, reminiscent of Giacometti sculptures.

"My workshop is like a best mate—always there for you when things get too much and life starts throwing things at you!"

The Saori Shed, as **Kim** calls her large, green wagon, sits in an open field in Norfolk, England, surrounded by farm buildings, pasture, and trees, as well as other sheds, all belonging to fellow artists and craftspeople. It is Kim's place of work and also a haven.

Resembling a trailer home more than anything, the shed started life as a 1967 Pilot Panloaf showman's wagon, complete with two pullout compartments on one side, which make it into a wider, more usable space. Originally, one pullout was a kitchen; the other, a living room. Their large windows bring great light into what is now Kim's workspace. She and her partner renovated the wagon, transforming it into a light and airy textiles studio.

Kim creates unique knitwear using the Japanese "freestyle" weaving technique of Saori, which has no rules or restrictions. The clothes that she makes can be worn in a number of ways so that many different looks can be created with just the one piece. She uses raw, local sheep's fleece, which she washes, dyes, and spins herself into "art yarns," then weaves them into her unique designs. Not only does Kim make the pieces herself, she teaches others how to as well.

To bring the shed to life, Kim painted the inside with vibrant colors, from a sunshine-yellow to a crimson-pink. The glossy wood veneer ceiling is still in place, complemented by the light wooden floor that Kim laid down. The cupboards, also original to the wagon, are used for storing the yarn. Skeins are arranged on shelves in a glorious rainbow of rich colors. The bathroom is now home to more equipment. A wood-burning stove, made by her partner's father in the 1970s, provides all the heating.

above left Set in a field, Kim's showman's wagon.

above right and inset Bold colors take visitors by surprise as they step inside the converted wagon, where Kim makes and sells her Saori knitwear. She has even upholstered the nursing chair with knitting.

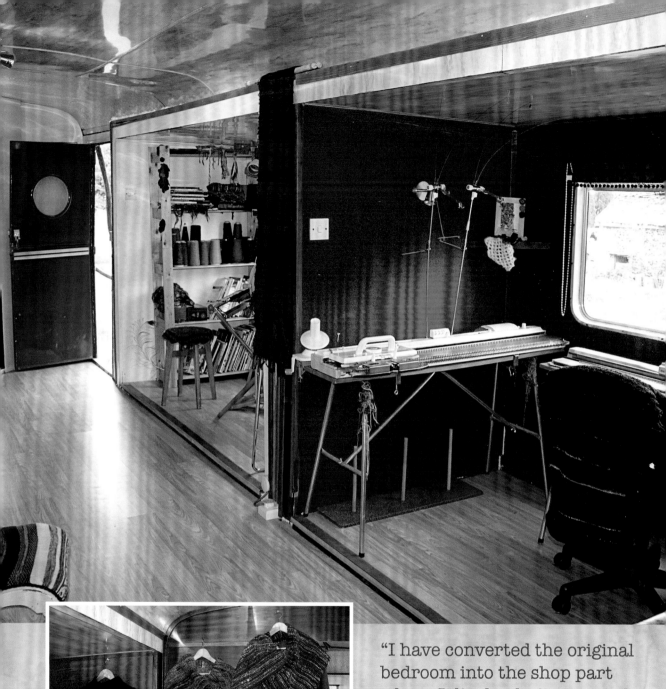

"I have converted the original bedroom into the shop part where I display knitwear and weaving equipment to inspire people who come to the Shed to experience the creative art of Japanese Saori weaving."

"Off I go, shifting shapes, collating colors. Snipping, tearing, drawing, painting, sticking—until the moment when something indirectly, or totally related, jumps out. Then I have a set of clear concepts and start to assemble. The results are truly joyful, challenging, and inspiring."

Having worked for years to strict deadlines and many a harsh brief in the speedy-needy world of advertising and design, in both London and Norfolk, **Maddy** started all over again, indulging her love of art and making.

Her powder-blue, clapboard shed stands in a miniature garden (yard), which is Maddy's tribute to the famous garden of the late filmmaker Derek Jarman, near Dungeness in Kent. Surrounded by shrubs and flowers, the shed is where she now turns her hand to making her creatures, tableaux, and collages.

There is everything that Maddy could possibly need inside to pursue her creative journey. Her desk, which sits under the window, is surrounded from floor to ceiling by a swirling assortment of natural and man-made objects—it is a delicious, tempting chaos of items that only she can locate, kept in an order that only she can understand. There are books, ribbons, maps, fabrics, feathers, papers, photographs, pebbles, paints, yarns, driftwood, chalk, beads, straw, string, and much, much more. The textures are mixed, the colors limitless. When Maddy starts on a project, she is never quite sure in which direction she will be taken, but that is exactly what makes the journey all the more fun.

above left Maddy has surrounded herself with all manner of objects to use in her making, from religious icons and royal photographs to an old violin and board games.

inset The shed's soothing powder-blue clapboard exterior and the tranquil setting are in direct contrast to the apparent chaos of the workspace.

above Standing almost precariously on stilts, Anne's corrugated tin studio was a Sunday school room in a nearby village. It was transported here in the late 1930s.

opposite The original tongue-and-groove walls have been painted white, and the ceiling a duck-egg blue, while the wooden floorboards, also original, have been left bare.

Tucked away in the hills on the Herefordshire side of the Welsh border is **Anne's** Sunday school room-turned-studio. Her home, a Primitive Methodist Chapel, is right next door. The house was built in 1867 at a time of social upheaval, when the difference between Church and Chapel in this part of the country accentuated the divisions in rural society.

Made of lightweight corrugated tin, the Sunday school room was easy to move from its original home in the hamlet of Lower Hergest, thirteen miles away, where it had fallen out of use. It was dismantled in 1937, brought here by horse and cart, and re-erected next to the chapel. Raised up on a timber frame, it looks over rolling hills, woods, and small fields, where sheep graze in all weathers.

From the outside, the Sunday school room appears to have changed very little, apart from some dents in the corrugated tin and a patina here and there of earthy red rust. Inside, there is basically one large room, although Anne added a bathroom in 2004. She has painted the original tongue-and-groove walls white, and the ceilings a duck-egg blue. The stepladder leads

"Sitting, staring, plotting, planning, doodling, drawing. Then making and doing and messing about..."

to a sleeping platform for Anne's nephews and other nimble guests, and a storage area.

Inspired by the wildlife and the surrounding landscape, Anne uses the Sunday school room as her studio, where she carries out every step involved In the creation of her amazing felt birds and animals, and, in fact, anything that belongs to the natural world. Some are lifesize, others outsize, such as the bird and animal masks she makes for various dramatic projects, including the entire cast of a Mad Hatter's Tea Party.

Tucked away in one corner are the oversized felt head of a hare and a robin lying flat on its back. They are so very lifelike but also quite unnerving, looking as if they're waiting to have life breathed into them. The same could be said of the heads of a barn owl and a crow, where the detailing is so exquisite, you feel as if they have feathers to stroke. Outside, where the steps lead down to the garden (yard), there are two doves perched on a branch. Such is the versatility of felt that Anne has, in her time, made boats, hats, boots, and even shrouds from it.

Down a slope, away from the chapel, is the pizza hut, a far cry from the ubiquitous franchise. This open-sided structure covers a pizza oven, which Anne sculpted out of clay and topped with a pewter coffee pot!

opposite above Rusty and patchworked, the old Sunday School shows signs of its age. Wood for the stove, the studio's only form of heating, is stored under a canopy of corrugated tin.

opposite below and inset A beautifully detailed dormouse mask for a Mad Hatter's Tea Party and a pair of doves, made from felt.

left The roof of the pizza hut is covered with succulents, so that it appears like an intrinsic part of the landscape.

This shed, overlooking the marshes at Shingle Street in Suffolk, England, combines a storage area for gardening tools and plant pots, and a separate studio. It was important to **Cee** to have this space to call her own and to do with it as she pleased, especially as her partner has her own studio in their shared beach house.

It was something of a challenge, both physically and emotionally, for Cee to get her shed. An earlier one had to be pulled down, and with that came the unenviable task of disposing of decades of paraphernalia that had been stored chock-a-block inside. Perhaps more difficult was Cee believing that she deserved to have her own creative space.

In this flat landscape, a beautiful vegetable and flower garden provides splashes of color against the weathered gray backdrop of

the clapboard shed. Cee helps them to survive the harsh sea winds by caring for them year-round, feeding, mulching, and protecting.

The studio is full of Cee's beach collections, personal treasures, and objects of inspiration. She uses this space for many creative activities, including making her willow baskets, examples of which hang from the rafters. At her table, she can draw and write, looking up from time to time over the water meadows on one side, the gorse and shingle landscape to the north, or into the vegetable garden. Or she might simply watch the birds or people passing, or practice t'ai chi.

"I've always had difficulty spending money on myself, supporting and taking seriously my creativity, and giving myself independent space separate from the shared house. I had to become more empowered and take charge of 'the new shed project.' Now I'm reaping the benefit of those struggles."

"This is where I sleep during the Glastonbury Festival, as I live in the village where it takes place, and I rent out the house."

above Candace displays made and found objects all over the garden.

opposite above Filled with the comforts of home, the shed is like a house in miniature.

opposite below The studio is an Aladdin's cave of delights.

In a small village of stone houses in Somerset, England, down a narrow land with a stream at the bottom of the hill, you come across a stone wall and a wooden gate. This leads to **Candace's** private world of house, garden (yard), and sheds.

Candace is a textile and mosaic artist and, as she lives in a fairly small house, the sheds are primarily extra rooms, each with its own particular role to play. At the far end of the garden stands her sky-blue painted shed, with its tiny porch. Named the "love shack" by a friend who spent her first night of married life in it with her new husband, this shed was originally a rather grand dog kennel. Since then, it's been lifted onto railroad ties (sleepers), and the wire mesh at the windows replaced with glass. The porch and the tin roof were also extended. Candace painted it blue outside and white inside, with a light green floor. In high summer, a beautiful white Rambling Rector rose trails over the roof.

Although small, this shed is like a home in miniature, with curtains at the windows, rugs on the floors, paintings on the walls, as well as robust furniture, including a folding bed with a feather mattress. Hanging from the ceiling is a wooden angel chandelier made by a friend. Everything about the space conveys a sense of welcome and a softness.

The stone structure at the top of the hill is Candace's mosaic studio, where she decorates mirrors, urns, shoes, and more with mosaics made from the stacks of china, much of it already broken. She has inserted Velux windows to provide her with enough natural light to work by. This space positively hums with creativity and industry. A trio of mosaic obelisks that Candace made, one pink, two blue, stand to attention outside.

"So, I sit and smile, play the music I choose, and I feel very good about what I am doing. It's a welcoming place for friends dropping by."

above The light-filled shed is ideal for Christina's work, creating stained-glass windows. One of Elena's designs, a sunburst retrieved from her partner's previous house, has found its way to their new home.

Light pours in through the stained glass window in the south-facing wall of **Christina's** shed in Norfolk, creating jewel-like pools on the vinyl floor. Christina's partner Elana retrieved the Art Deco-style semicircle, which she had made, from above the front door of her London home when she sold it (the new owners were going to get rid of it). It is a unique and colorful reminder of her house before she and Elana set up home together in Norfolk.

As the sun moves from east to west, the light travels along the sky-blue wall. A Venetian blind at the window beneath the stained glass helps to keep out the glare and the temperatures down. At the height of summer, the double glazed doors remain open all day.

Christina and Elana created this charming clapboard shed with its overhanging roof and small stoep, or colonial-style veranda, to remind them of the happy times they had when living in Africa—Elana was brought up in Zimbabwe, Christina worked in West Africa, and they ended up in South Africa before they moved to England. The space gives Christina all she could wish for in a studio. She has room to spread out when she creates her own stained glass designs. Her materials are all close to hand, with sheets of glass in a myriad colors stored in a compartmented shelf. When she needs to take a breather from work, she can sit on the stoep in one of the chairs and take in the view across their lovely garden to the pond, and the trees beyond.

above With its veranda and overhanging roof, Christina's shed has a colonial look about it, bringing back sweet memories of the time she lived in Africa.

"I dip in and out of the workshop with indigo-dyed clothy blue fingers, unwrapping the little packets of bound silky watching the color change as the air touches them. This is the best time in my indoors/outdoors space."

In summer, **Jenny's** plain wooden shed in Suffolk, England, is transformed by the jumble of honeysuckle, clematis, and roses that cascades down, almost obscuring the door. A well-kept border of cottage garden plants rises up to meet it. Inside, the shed is a similarly busy jumble of all the materials Jenny uses in her work.

The shed reflects Jenny's diverse artistic activities. She is first and foremost a textile artist, making wonderful scarves and cloths that she sells at craft markets and in Craftco, a co-operative craft store nearby, in the coastal town of Southwold, Suffolk, England. Stacks of transparent boxes keep fabrics clean and tidy, but at the same time in clear view, while an old wooden plan chest stores paper and card pristine and flat. Shelves are crammed full, too, of various odds and ends.

The scene inside the shed appears rather disorderly but Jenny knows exactly what she has and where to find it. She is a keen collector and sees the value in objects that others might ignore. She turns various recycled materials, such as bags of coffee, into extraordinary bags, and she also leads workshops in the community and in schools for which she always needs an array of materials, from dried leaves and willow to plastic bags and telephone wire.

There is no water in the shed, so Jenny is always moving back and forth between here and the kitchen, sometimes for work, sometimes to make a cup of tea or her lunch. As she passes through the garden (yard), she is always distracted by something—birds and insects, perhaps, or plants that need watering. At times she simply stands still and gazes across the fields.

Sunny days see Jenny dyeing her cloth in the garden. She particularly enjoys working with indigo and is drawn to the strange and compelling smell that comes from the dye vat. She also never tires of seeing the unpredictable depth of color developing in the cloth.

opposite The shed is transformed in summer as roses, honeysuckle, and clematis clamber their way over the roof.

above left and right The shelves are bursting with craft materials as well as works in progress.

below Colored threads, stored in an open drawer, wait their turn to be incorporated in one of Jenny's creations.

Chapter 4

Sheds **for sculptors and potters**

It could be said that a sculptor's or a potter's shed is more like a workshop than a studio. There has to be space and light in which to create, and also somewhere to keep half-finished pieces and work ready for sale, as well as found objects used for inspiration. But there also has to be storage for tools and materials, machinery and molds, sometimes even welding equipment, hoists, and so on.

With such activity going on inside, these sheds used for sculpture or pottery can be cluttered, dirty places with cement dust, stone dust, wood dust on surfaces or they can be light, white, clean, and pristine.

Standard sheds are often simply not big enough, as the work created inside may be too tall or too bulky to fit. Space might be needed to see the work from a distance and to photograph it, and different areas may be needed for the various stages of production. And then there should always be somewhere to sit, draw, socialize, and think.

Charlotte is a sculptor and letter carver, who now does all her work in the shed, which she had built at the end of her north London garden (yard) about two years ago. She longed for a light and airy place to call her own, where she could work in peace and quiet, uninterrupted by children and footballs.

This space is truly hers, filled with her books, her tools, with her music playing—all very liberating and good for creativity. She also doesn't have to worry about tidying away her work when she finishes, and everything remains exactly as she leaves it for the next day. The rest of the family are also very happy about the turn of events—they no longer have reason to complain about all the dust she used to make.

A great deal of thought was put into the design of the studio, so that it would fit well into its surroundings. The brick exterior complements the row houses that run front and back, while the floor-to-ceiling glass doors reflect those of Charlotte's kitchen. Meanwhile, the floor tiles echo those outside, bringing a sense of continuity between inside and out. There are both electricity and water supplies to the shed, and a butler's sink has been plumbed in for washing tools, cloths, and hands.

above One of Charlotte's stone letter carvings stands on the large easel, together with her sketches and tools.

below Smaller pieces can be carved at the pine workbench.

opposite Made from the same materials as the surrounding houses, the brick-built shed, with its floor-to-ceiling glass doors, stands comfortably in this city space.

"I now have somewhere with my choice of music, my picture that Ben hates on the wall, my carving stuff, reference books, notebooks, and my thoughts."

Charlotte carves on a large easel, but for small pieces works directly on her pine workbench. A bench dog, lipped at the front and back, holds the stone in place and prevents it slipping. Above the workbench is a wall-hung cabinet where Charlotte keeps all her books and reference materials free from dust when she's hard at work with the chisel. A portable radio—her constant companion—tuned into her favorite music station, stands on top of an old printer's box found at an auction some years ago.

The first carving that Charlotte made here with her name "Ruse" inscribed is laid into the brick wall outside the studio. Visible through the greenery, leaning against the rock wall, is a piece of Lakeland stone carved with the words "Hard Place"—a nod to the saying, "Between a rock and a hard place."

As well as working in the classical style, Charlotte enjoys mixing urban art styles with traditional letter carving, using comics and graphic novels for reference. She likes to see how an essentially throwaway art form such as graffiti can be set forever in stone. Accordingly, she has spent many an hour in the shed creating visual puns that break traditional rules.

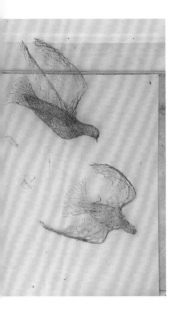

After working for many years as a printmaker and sculptor, **Jenny** is now channeling her creativity into wirework, using her hands to push, pinch, and mold wire into life. Her pieces range from life-size animals to small table sculptures. Ghost-like, her creations graze and haunt her world temporarily on their way to new homes in other gardens (yards) and galleries.

Her eight-sided shed is probably as far away from her Suffolk, England, house as it could be—the other side of a field and reached by a small, slatted wood bridge. Being detached from home, both physically and mentally, is crucial to her creativity—before the shed, which she bought with an inheritance, she worked at the family kitchen table.

For the small, simple shapes like birds, Jenny works the wire inside the shed, using a pinboard on which she "sketches" with the wire until they can be complete pieces. The shed isn't big enough, though, to make her larger pieces, such as horses. She creates these outdoors from rolls of galvanized wire, which doesn't rust. As she works she is often kept company by a finished piece, a ghostly apparition, such as the woman sitting on the bench reading.

From the outside, the shed, with its tall windows, looks like a summerhouse to which you might be invited to take afternoon tea. It is painted a sophisticated pale lilac, with the inside a creamy white, and there are even muslin drapes hanging at the windows. Appearances are, in this case, deceptive. The shed is a purely functional space, filled with all the tools and paraphernalia that Jenny needs to pursue her craft.

above and inset The life-size figure of a woman, one of Jenny's galvanized wire creations, sits ghost-like on a bench outside the shed.

opposite, above left Intricately detailed wirework pigeons, discreetly pinned, appear to swoop across the wall.

"Having worked all my life on the kitchen table, the shed seemed, at first, too pristine to use as a studio, more appropriate for a calm sit down with a glass of something. However, work in progress has now filled every corner and I am joined by the cat, Jago the lurcher, and several chickens, who enjoy sunbathing on the mat."

above The newest and largest of Bridget's sheds is her studio, where she sculpts. The smaller shed alongside contains her etching press.

opposite and inset With a partly translucent roof, the studio is filled with natural light, making it perfect for working in and for displaying works of balsa, card, clay, and bronze. Bridget's tools of the trade are also kept here, in full view.

From the outside, **Bridget's** house at the end of a row looks pretty much like all the others in her street. But when you venture inside, you know you are in for a treat. Her home is full of creativity, books, and beauty.

Together with its sheds, the house is situated on one of the quays at Great Yarmouth, in Suffolk, England. Not so very long ago this fishing port housed an industry that employed thousands of men and women and was crammed with herring boats. Sadly, that is now all gone.

Bridget has always had a collection of sheds in her garden (yard) dedicated to her work. She pulled two of them down fairly recently because they weren't big enough and also let in the rain. In their place, she built a new, bigger one, to be her studio. With large windows and a translucent cover for half the roof, it is specifically designed for space and light. There are buckets, shelves, and tables with tools laid out on them. Work in progress and finished pieces waiting to be exhibited, made out of balsa and cardboard, clay and bronze, are either in repose on plinths or partying on the specially built shelves that run around the perimeter.

The shed alongside the studio houses Bridget's etching press. It is darker than the studio, but small and easier to keep warm. A third, much smaller shed, belonging to the original building, is where Bridget stores foundry moulds, armatures, and other bulky things for supporting her work.

Bridget also uses the house and garden for displaying finished work. Just outside the studio, in the shade of a tree, an almost life-size male bronze nude sits looking out over flowers and vegetables and more sculptures. The garden is alive with the sound of birds, especially starlings, which give Bridget endless pleasure.

"It's strange but once I am in the studio I feel completely at home in the world. I live and work alone, which means I can move between studio and house as and when I please, with no heed to time or mess."

above left Examples of Elspeth's work are lined up on this long table, where she coaxes clay into various shapes. Pitchers and vases filled with teasels and dried flowers and grasses make a decorative backdrop.

above center Once a local cricket team's pavilion, this wooden shed is now Elspeth's pottery studio.

above right From time to time, Elspeth welcomes the public into her studio, and exhibits her work on on a long wooden table. Shown here are curves of clay which are part of "Axis of Dancing," conveying a sense of a backbone.

When **Elspeth** stumbled across this wooden shed in Cambridgeshire, England, it was beginning to rot, many of the windows were broken, and house martins were nesting inside. Taking on the building, which had been the Grantchester cricket team's pavilion, was a major step but Elspeth knew that it would make the perfect pottery studio. Still working here after thirty-five years, she obviously made the right decision.

Elspeth has a deep connection to the pavilion and its surroundings. It is her place of belonging, and safety, and a life-long companion. Along the way, it has shared in the ideas, conceptions, and manifestations of her imagination, but also fed her creativity.

This wooden palace seems to have a will of its own, and Elspeth believes that it will stand here as long as it chooses, offering shelter and inspiration to any who come by. She acknowledges that it has skillfully eluded her control by "breathing, stretching, creaking, and smelling variously over the years." Accordingly, she has made only basic repairs to the building and willingly accepts the companionship of mice, which make their nests here, and spiders, which spin their webs.

"Here I can listen to the little owl in the old walnut tree beside me... I can hear the motorway not far off and the boy racers that defy the speed limit on their bikes through the village. Thank you shed of my dreams, for coming into my life."

For Elspeth, the shed is a working studio but she does open it to the public from time to time. When exhibiting, she lays out her clay pots among found objects on tables. The bare floorboards match the original tongue-and-groove paneled walls, on which she hangs notes, photographs, and pictures for inspiration. At one end is a potter's workbench, cupboards for all her equipment, tubs of clay, and a tabletop oven, where some of the alchemy takes place. Using basic potting methods of pinching and hollowing or rolling and shaping, low-temperature firing and waxing Elspeth creates simple shapes that are alive with the intention and touch she brings to them. As she works, she "shapes and rolls and smooths the clay over and over again to make pots and other forms that can leave the hut and become the companions of others."

"I still go and make pots in mine, and maybe I'll grow to like it more as the months pass. In fact I'm feeling rather guilty about my negative attitude to my poor shed. I must go and reassure it that it's not really at all unlovable—I'm the problem."

This is a tale of two sheds, and about love, creativity, and loss, from a time when **Bay** was yet to move, leaving her sheds behind, to embark on a new journey, taking her cherished memories with her.

Bay's shed, small and efficient, was tucked away behind her house in Exeter, England. In this purely functional space, she created her beautifully glazed pottery. The tools of her trade lay in wait on tables and shelves, to be used to form bowls, cups, and other shapes in assorted hues. Her kiln and two potter's wheels were kept here, too, together with a wooden wedging table and a large sink with a plentiful supply of hot water. Glaze buckets were stacked on the floor, and the shelves held pots that were drying and waiting to be finished.

Her husband Patrick's shed was functional as well, but, unlike Bay's, it was a place of beauty, created from his imagination. For him, it was a place to paint and draw, listen to music on the record player, and recline and contemplate his work.

When Patrick died, his shed became Bay's, and she found it difficult to talk about her own shed when Patrick's held such meaning for her. She wrote, at the time, "I'm sitting next to it now, on the deck. It doesn't feel empty or unused, just a place of calm creativity and contentment."

She would sometimes lie on the bed in Patrick's shed and doze as she remembered her lovely man and all of their years together. Her heart was here, with his paintings and drawings on the wall, and his LPs scattered on top of an old cupboard.

Bay never really loved her shed, not in the way she loved Patrick's. It wasn't a place of refuge and retreat, where she could feel truly herself. It was more a place of work, where she made her pots, taught students, and entertained grandchildren, helping them to make their latest craze in clay.

In spite of the love and loss and longing, there were pots still to be made, and Bay tried to like her shed more. Since then, Bay has moved on, away from the home that she and Patrick shared, to be by the sea, with her family close by. In a new shed, she will be creating pots once more.

opposite above Bay loved Patrick's weathered clapboard shed simply because it was his. After his death, it became her refuge and retreat.

opposite below Some of Bay's glazed pots were used to store pencils, brushes, and modeling tools used for her work.

above Bay's shed was always a practical, working space, where she made her pots. Although similar in use of materials to Patrick's, she never felt the same emotional attachment to it.

Maddy has traveled extensively with her work as an artist and a sculptor, finding inspiration in the deserts of California, Colorado, and Nevada, the lakes of Vermont, and the coasts of Maine, Massachusetts, and Rhode Island. Two years ago, she settled in Westport, Massachusetts.

From a distance, her cedar shingle studio resembles a modest house. But as you approach, you notice two "up-and-over" doors facing each other. When rolled back, they transform the space, making it lighter and more open, while creating a through breeze.

Maddy works at a large functional table in the center of the studio, and around it, the concrete floor is splashed with paint. The interior walls are made of plywood and boards of Homasote (recycled cellulose fiber), which allow her to nail or screw into them wherever she chooses, to display her work. Making the most of such a large area, Maddy has included a space for relaxation, made up of two retro car seats and a low table. There's also a kitchenette, equipped with a tea kettle and a sink, and a bathroom.

Maddy designed and built her studio with the express purpose of making, looking at, and thinking about line, color, and shape, free from the interruptions of family, phones, or meals. Some friends refer to it as her sanctuary but, to Maddy, it's simply a place of quiet where she can work. Here, she feels that she has truly found her place, and for that she is most grateful.

"My studio is a place where I feel a calm [free] from all expectations. It is a hub of quiet in a noisy life of expectations, goals, responsibilities. I choose to live in a farming and fishing village with no ambient light or noise except the roar of my neighbors' diesel truck every morning at 7 a.m. It beats an alarm clock or a rooster."

above Maddy loves to scour the nearby beach after a storm for flotsam and jestsam to use in her art. Examples of it hang from the studio walls.

inset When rolled back, the "up-and-over" doors in the cedar shingle studio create an open, airy space.

Chapter 5

Sheds **for growers**

Women have always grown, processed, marketed, and prepared food. Often, as a result of tradition or necessity, they are custodians of their land and its native plants. For some women, their vegetable gardens give them and their family a measure of food security.

But women also grow for pleasure, to provide the kitchen with the freshest, tastiest, and most nutritious produce possible. They may have ethical and health concerns about big business, food miles, chemicals, and G.M. modification but, by growing their own, they can be sure their fruit and vegetables are produced in accordance with their beliefs.

For others, the veggie patch is about the smaller picture, planting for butterflies and bees, making ponds for wildlife, and planting to control pests. It's a place to get away from it all—away from the domestic sphere, from work, from families—and be immersed in seeds and seasons, in sowing, planting, and harvesting.

The shed plays a crucial role in growing your own. It's where tools, seeds, and other gardening paraphernalia that make it all possible are stored. But it can also be a retreat, complete with a table and chairs, a stove, and a tea kettle.

Note: many of the women featured in this chapter are from the U.K. and have allotments, which are plots of usually public land, rented on an individual basis for cultivation. The nearest equivalent in the U.S.A. is the community garden, which is shared and usually farmed collectively.

above and inset In her peaceful garden shed, surrounded by trees and shrubs, Fiona can leave behind the cares of the world. On warm nights, lit by candles, it makes the perfect setting for guests.

opposite The allotment shed, shaped like a railroad wagon, has a more practical purpose, storing gardening equipment, but with its comfy chairs, it is also a place for daydreaming.

Fiona has two sheds: one in the small garden of her home in Norwich, England, and the other on her allotment on the outskirts of the city.

Fiona gifted these sheds to herself at key points in her life, sensing that they might fulfill some important need, which they do. Although very different in style, they both allow her to indulge a wish for solitude, to forget the demands of domesticity, and to be surrounded by the natural world. They are her escape to a different, more intense reality, where time slows right down.

The former is more like a garden room, positioned at the end of a winding path, where it catches the late afternoon sun. Camouflaged by mature trees and shrubs, it is an oasis of calm. There are lots of windows and a glazed door, so even when inside, there is always the feeling of being at one with nature.

Hidden away from the house, the shed can be a place for solitude or, when the doors are thrown open to the courtyard, the ideal spot for socializing and partying. Inside, there are a wicker sofa with cushions and a wicker chair for relaxation, together with a metal table and folding chairs that look out onto the garden. Decorating one corner of the cream tongue-and-groove walls is a cluster of postcards, happy reminders of places visited by Fiona and her friends.

The second shed, at the top end of her plot, faces west, perfect for experiencing the spectacular city sunsets. Inspired by a childhood memory, Fiona hankered after a shed shaped like a railroad wagon. Her builder was happy to oblige and constructed a basic timber-framed and planked shed with a curved corrugated roof.

This is Fiona's working shed, where she sorts and stores seeds, chits potatoes, and gazes out onto her plot, deciding what to plant, to weed, and to harvest throughout the year. Well-looked-after spades and forks hang from the walls, while smaller tools and gardening equipment are kept in drawers. Making the space altogether cozier are a comfy armchair and a spare chair for visitors, and two paintings on the wall. Two chests of drawers—one looking rather posh for a shed—are used to store odds and ends. In one corner there is a gas burner and everything she needs to make a pot of tea. Here, she can sit and daydream. In forgetting the preoccupations of the day, she can connect with what really matters in her life.

"I think my sheds answer to some very deep primal urge within me, some ancient 'call to the wild' or as close as I can get to it on a daily basis."

Trish has two allotment plots side by side, both with sheds, on the coast in Norfolk, England. All her neighbors have sheds, too, and it is quite difficult to see where her plots and those of her neighbors begin and end.

The local terrain and weather are the motivation behind what Trish chooses to grow, and she delights in discovering the best way of producing organic food all year round. She experiments with rotation techniques, to discover the most suitable places for the various crops. She sows heritage seeds, and grows several types of each vegetable, in order to find the best performers and to guard against failure. Many of her herbs and vegetables produce edible flowers, which she sells to the local Michelin-starred restaurant, to decorate its dishes.

Trish has greenhouses and fruit cages on both plots, to protect and nurture her crops, while her sheds are for storage, potting up plants, and puttering about. Wonderfully hotchpotch in their construction, they are made from old windows and doors, corrugated iron, and scrap timber.

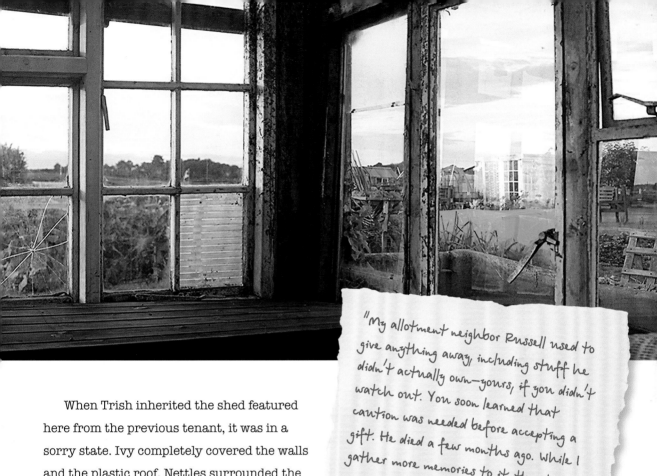

When Trish inherited the shed featured here from the previous tenant, it was in a sorry state. Ivy completely covered the walls and the plastic roof. Nettles surrounded the base and were creeping under the rotten walls at the bottom. Inside, there was a sizeable mallow taking up valuable space. Desiccated rat skeletons and a rabbit hole, down which Alice might easily have fallen, were revealed when the decaying door used as a bench was heaved to one side. Although the skeletons and the mallow are long gone, the shed remains much as it was, which gives it its charm.

Sitting in one of the two very rickety chairs in the shed, Trish can gaze out over her plot and those of her neighbors to the fields beyond. After sowing seeds into trays perched on her lap, she then moves them to a very rough old bench. Here, the plants soak up the sun through the cobwebby windows until the day they are big enough to be potted on or planted outside in newly prepared and rotated beds.

"My allotment neighbor Russell used to give anything away, including stuff he didn't actually own—yours, if you didn't watch out. You soon learned that caution was needed before accepting a gift. He died a few months ago. While I gather more memories to it, the shed means Russell's company to me. I even miss him nicking [taking] my raspberries."

opposite above Tools are lined up neatly, ready to use, against the clay lump wall of the shed. The ivy growing outside, almost obscuring the window, provides food and shelter for birds and butterflies.

left In spring and summer, the hoophouses come into use, protecting grapes and vegetables from the birds.

bottom left Apples in wooden crates are among the crops stored in the shed over winter.

bottom right Ivy creeps stealthily upward, colonizing the inside of the shed as well.

When we visited **Marion**, she was just back from a farmer's market with empty and near-empty boxes. Her farm is her business and her passion. Marion's produce is organic, local, and fresh. She has a hoophouse (polytunnel) and an old outbuilding, which is her working shed. Inside, there are boxes filled with this season's crops. From a beam hang onions woven into beautiful strings. As visitors to her farmhouse kitchen in Suffolk, England, we were offered coffee and sweet, sticky "dried" pears from her orchard, which had been left overnight in the solid-fuel stove—delicious!

In spring, birds fly around the shed; usually there's a nest of wrens, sometimes sparrows, and the adults flit in and out. But the spring is also a time of frenetic activity in the garden, which sees Marion grabbing tools at every opportunity, filling seed trays and pots, sieving potting compost, and writing labels.

Marion's shed contains netting and homemade cloches to protect crops from unwelcome visitors, watering cans and sprinklers, stones for sharpening knives and tools, string for supports, clippers for pruning, and fleece to protect plants from the late frosts.

In summer, the shed is filled with early crops of autumn-sown onions and garlic, potted-up treasures from roadside stalls, and surplus plants to share with friends. Outside, a blackbird calls joyfully from the rooftop, and the peach tree against the south-facing front wall has 88 peaches ready to be picked.

Fall is the serious harvesting time: the shed fills up with baskets and boxes of onions, potatoes, squash, and fruit. With the approach of colder weather, the crops are covered again but it will not be long before the propagator comes out for next year's produce.

Kerina's woodsheds in Suffolk, England, with their rusty corrugated tin roofs, sit side by side at the edge of a small mature wood—mainly ash, oak, hazel, aspen, holly, and elm—that she owns. One is full of machinery and everything Kerina needs to manage the woodland. In the other, she cuts and stores wood in the dry for her cast-iron stove at home, which provides her heating.

Although it has an entirely practical purpose, the shed does hold a great significance for Kerina. She loves the time spent filling it, dragging her quarry back from the wood, which she either harvests from living trees in winter before the sap rises or from dead branches lying on the ground. The absolute simplicity of the task allows her to relax and think while felling, gathering, sorting, and cutting. There is pleasure, too, in seeing the log pile at the back of her shed gradually grow, in the knowledge that she will stay warm over the winter.

When the weather is fine, Kerina cuts the wood outside, but if it's raining, she brings her chainsaw and sawhorse under cover. Inside the shed, she's also allocated a space for storing wood that needs to dry before being cut into stove-sized pieces for burning. Logs too big to be kept here, and which need much longer before they are seasoned, she piles up behind the shed for cutting the following year.

left and inset Kerina's two sheds, side by side, may look like they need a few repairs but they are still fit for purpose. In the open-fronted shed she stores and cuts wood with a chainsaw, but when the sun shines, she brings the sawhorse outside.

Jude has two sheds in her garden in Suffolk, England. The one featured here is an old brick outhouse, or privy, which is just big enough for Jude, a keen gardener, to use as a potting shed and nurture her plants. Further up the garden is her second shed, an altogether different kind of place, where she nurtures herself.

When Jude first set foot inside the outhouse there was still a plank of wood in place, with three holes neatly cut in a row—two large ones for adults and one small for a child—balanced over three old metal buckets. She wondered if the original family ever sat there together and chatted!

Jude is very fond of her old outhouse. In summer, the red-brick walls and tiled roof are covered in honeysuckle and huge and wondrous white climbing roses. These continue heavenward into the overhanging trees, filling the air with wafts of scent. A rustic wooden seat faces the sun, perfect for resting, thinking, and enjoying a cup of tea with a friend.

Behind the faded blue-green painted door, the shed is quite unprepossessing—it's simply somewhere for Jude to store her garden tools and old pots. She freely admits that it's rather dank, dark, and cold, and often untidy. In the spring, she sorts out the pots, sweeps the floor, and generally clean things up. With order restored, she enjoys potting up her plants.

opposite and inset With nothing new used in its construction, this shed is an excellent example of recycling.

right Outside the shed, where clematis grows up against its faded green walls, the vintage bench provides welcome breaks from tending the vegetable beds.

This clapboard shed is a fine example of recycling. **Marian** built it in her garden (yard) in Suffolk, England, with her friend Nicolette. It involved a huge amount of planning, which all paid off—the actual construction took just two weeks. Marian collected all the recycled materials she needed herself, including old windows and timber left over after renovating the house, bits of cladding acquired after hours of patient bidding at the local auction house, and an old door from a friend's barn.

Inside, the shed is filled to the gunwales with all the paraphernalia required by these two very keen and knowledgeable gardeners. According to their deeply held beliefs, the produce from their abundant garden is organically grown, and it provides enough food—and pleasure—for most of the year, so much so that some of it is sold in Marian's health food store in a nearby town.

With the shed comes the added satisfaction for Marian of knowing that she created it from scratch. Indeed, why would anyone buy one off-the-shelf if they have the time, imagination, and resourcefulness to make one for themselves?

Time and the elements have weathered this shed beautifully so it appears as if it has always belonged. Every time Marian looks at it now, sees it from another angle, or in a different light, it makes her smile.

opposite and inset right
This tiny shed has a big personality, with its blue paintwork and African-inspired patterns around the door and along the sides. In strong sunlight, the paint takes on a lighter hue.

far right Belying its colorful exterior, the inside of the shed is undecorated and is a purely functional space.

In her vegetable garden, in the midst of a rural Suffolk, England, farm, Lindsay has created a Caribbean splash of vibrant blue, painting her tiny shed, which she rescued from a bonfire before it went up in flames. It makes a bold statement in among the muted English colors of the surrounding fields and woodland.

The paint was expensive and **Lindsay** wondered if she had been rash to buy it. However, it has proved a wise investment, having held season after season. Unfortunately, the color was not to everyone's taste, upsetting one of Lindsay's neighbors, so she simply painted the back of it a tasteful green and all was well again!

The motifs around the doors and windows are stencils, which Lindsay cut out from an old bath mat. They are based on West African "lozenge" patterns, of overlapping triangular designs found on fabrics and rugs. These patterns also decorate her djembe drum, which was actually the inspiration behind the shed's decoration.

With its jolly coat of paint on the outside, the shed interior is purely practical. It is where Lindsay keeps all her tools for the vegetable garden, the rakes, spades, and hoes leaning against the wall, and fertilizers and trowels stored on the shelves.

"For me, this shed represents a world of ancient smells, hay, milk, and straw... It is a lovely place that all the sheep and goats are fond of."

Claude's picturesque farm is nestled among hills in the La Sarthe region of northwest France. Horses, sheep, lambs, and goats live a contented life in the small fields. A disused railway track crosses the land, which the goats used to walk along like dogs, until they became too wayward. Closer to the farmhouse, a peacock roams freely, screeching its eerie cry.

There are a number of sheds scattered around the farm—for storage, chickens, machinery, and tools—but it is the ewes' shed that draws the eye. It has a particular charm all of its own, sitting under the trees at the bottom of a hilly field.

Unchanged since it was built many years ago, long before Claude and her partner bought the farm, this simple and unadorned wooden shed symbolizes the beginning of life. At night or early in the morning when it's still dark, it helps to reassure a ewe about to lamb. In tune with its surroundings, this is a peaceful place, where all the animals feel protected.

Down a long and winding lane, through the woods and hills of a Somerset, England, landscape, lies **Dee's** smallholding, where she lives in attendance on her sheep and pigs, and grows fruit and vegetables.

Dee's journey to this point has not been an easy one. Her simple, no-frills way of life upset a few people and she experienced some local opposition, that is until a local architect championed her, taking on the "system." Eventually, she was granted planning permission to live her life as she chose—in a trailer (mobile home) on her land.

Although understandably suspicious of outsiders, Dee was warm and welcoming, and with a sharp mind and wit. She related her tale of how she came to be here and her hopes for the future. For the first four years, she lived in one of her sheds. Inside, she created a small kitchen and slept on a fold-up bed, which she had to tidy away each morning. The shower comprised a watering can, and the runoff was caught in a bowl and used to water the garden. Wool from her own sheep lined the walls, and there was a little wood burner for when it was really cold.

Dee is trying to be as self-sufficient as possible: growing vegetables; keeping pigs for sausages, bacon, and gammon; sheep for lambs and the cooking pot; and chickens for eggs. She has planted many trees and, with luck, will see them mature and produce fruit. She hopes her land, her trailer, and her sheds will see her through the rest of her days.

Robyn is one of many younger women who has taken on an allotment for the satisfaction of growing food for the family—in this case, for her and her partner. Most days, she comes here after work to pick a few peas and beans, or whatever else is ready, for supper.

Her plot is one of many similar neat ones in a field of allotments in Suffolk, England, and her unassuming shed, small and wooden, has a purely practical use. Robyn stores all her gardening equipment here, from large plastic buckets for gathering weeds to slug pellets, from a metal burner to a wheelbarrow, and a few rolls of toilet paper, just in case! She shelters in here when it's wet and also when the sun is blazing down. There are no windows, so in driving rain she will stand just inside, holding the door nearly closed, and peer out at the weather while staying dry.

On occasions, the odd small creature finds its way inside the shed—in winter, she often finds snails living in the sleeves of her mac—but Robyn has no problem about them sharing her space or, indeed, how untidy it sometimes gets. What is important to her is that her shed gives her a feeling of permanence and belonging.

inset All Robyn's allotment tools are stored in the shed, so it's easy to make spur-of-the-moment visits.

right The shed presides over a well-tended allotment, which provides year-round vegetables for the table.

"I don't want to feel like a visitor, carrying my tools with me and taking them away again each time. I like the fact that my shed doesn't have to be beautiful, clean or tidy."

"We built the shed, my boyfriend and I, and found out how well we worked together. Our foundation was strong."

When **Sarah's** boyfriend moved into her home in Ipswich, Massachusetts, she let him use the garage for storage. But her heart sank as the space filled up with boxes and musical equipment, old furniture, and clothes. Suddenly, she realized she had no place to store all her gardening tools and pots. Every time she looked for her favorite spade or hauled the lawnmower out of its new home in the basement, she longed for a shed of her own.

Finding that shed went to the top of her to-do list, and over the course of the summer, she did her research, hoping to find one that would meet her needs exactly. She discussed features such as door widths, types of hooks, and so on with friends, and she looked at all sorts of prebuilt sheds, but found them much too fancy and expensive. By the fall, she realized that she would have to build the shed herself—with the help of her boyfriend, who, fortune would have it, is a carpenter. This barn-like shed, with its white-painted cedar shingles and dark green trim and double doors, has a definite New England look about it. Hanging outside the sash window is a window box planted up with red pelargoniums, adding to the charm. Inside, the shed is exactly as Sarah intended: nothing more, nothing less than a place for her tools; a space to call her own.

left and inset Sarah's cedar shingle shed, painted white and with dark green double doors and trim, stands serenely in the yard. Designed to her specifications and filled with her tools, it is an extremely tidy space.

below Using locally manufactured and recycled materials such as roof and flooring tiles, Catherine has restored the half-timbered barn to its former glory.

opposite above The lean-to attached to the barn was in a chronic state of disrepair but Catherine restored that too, creating a studio and dining room.

opposite below Even the donkeys have their own shed.

Chickens, a dog, and a number of cats roam **Catherine's** smallholding more or less at will. Situated in a remote part of La Sarthe in northwest France, it includes a vegetable garden, donkey paddock, and a large, restored barn, which is her shed.

When Catherine bought the farm, the barn was scarcely standing. Just a fraction of its original half-timbering remained, with most of the walls made of rusty corrugated iron. Over time, she brought the barn back to life, restoring the half-timbering and rebuilding the roof. In keeping with the age of the barn, she used locally manufactured tiles, timber, roof, and flooring tiles reclaimed from old demolished buildings.

She has divided up the space into small rooms, where she stores tools, garden equipment, and wood for her fire, as well as undertaking home improvements. With an eye on cost and the age of the barn, she has used old greenhouse glass for the windows sandwiched in between the half-timbering. Similarly, the exterior doors came from an Emmaus charitable community where

opposite above Wire mesh replaces the wooden panels in the fitted cupboard to make a cabinet of curiosities, displaying treasures and mementoes.

opposite below Chopped logs and bunches of twigs in the wood shed are stored ready for use Sharing two of the barn's walls, the shed is otherwise exposed to the elements.

left and below Various decorative touches, such as crucifixes, a rug, and a birdcage, add personality to the functional spaces within the barn.

above right At the back of the barn is the lean-to chicken coop.

secondhand and recyclables are sold. Discarded apartment doors, dating back to the mid-nineteenth century, were rescued from the streets of Paris by Catherine's friend Rémy, and look completely at home dividing up the barn interior.

Catherine has turned a very dilapidated lean-to, whose roof and walls were covered with rusty corrugated iron, into a studio and dining room overlooking the garden. She uses the space to entertain but also to enjoy the peace and quiet, painting or gazing out onto the garden and the pond. From here, she can keep an eye on her three donkeys in their paddock. They have their own shed, for sleeping and sheltering from the elements and the flies.

A cupboard constructed by Rémy, and Colette, whose shed is featured on pages 192–5, has had its panels replaced with wire mesh. It now acts as a cabinet of curiosities. Meanwhile, installed in the old stables, is an enormous, old wooden larder, reclaimed from a butcher's shop. It's now used for storing all sorts of provisions, including jams, vegetables, bottles of wine...

Jessica picked up the phone one day when her husband was out and ordered a shed. She didn't tell him about the call and, when the shed was delivered, he was far from pleased. For Jessica, though, the shed was a statement and marked a significant new beginning in her life.

Jessica, a keen weekend gardener, said that she should have known her marriage was in trouble when she no longer felt like sharing the existing shed with her husband. He had firmly stamped his mark on it, filling it with building materials, hammers and wrenches, jars and jars of nails, screws, and drill-bits. The subtle trappings of her hobby, such as seed packets, stakes, and twine, had no place there, overpowered by all the masculine hardware.

"I needed my own garden shed. It was a moment of reckoning."

Perhaps not to provoke her husband, Jessica chose a shed that was small and unobtrusive. She tucked it away in the corner of their property on the shore of Hardys Creek, a tributary of the Essex River in Massachusetts. It was as far away from his shed and the house as it could possibly be. In buying her shed, Jessica felt that she was taking control of her own life. It was an act of bravery, and once she had taken this step, she was able to move on with her life and move her husband out. With the marriage over, both sheds were now hers.

For the time being, his shed stands empty, waiting for Jessica to do with it exactly as she chooses. In the meantime, hers is filled with the stuff of the living, from cat carriers and garden furniture to off-season clothes and birdseed.

opposite A symbol of Jessica's discontent, her husband's shed, situated close to the house and filled with power tools, was everything she didn't want her shed to be.

above In contrast, Jessica's secluded shed, set in a far corner of the garden, symbolizes her new-found independence and happiness. It is filled with everything she needs for her gardening.

Laura lives next to the farm that her family has run for a very long time. Her mother, Meredith, whose shed is featured on pages 68–9, and her father live two doors away. Nature is all around. Both properties, close to the Massachusetts town of Ipswich, are surrounded by mature forest, large rocks, and salt marshes. There are coyotes and wolves in a nearby education centre, crickets, and an abundance of birds, including beautiful hummingbirds—and mosquitoes.

Laura's shed was intended to be purely practical. It was somewhere to keep her chickens and their feed, gardening tools, and equipment. But when two miniature stallions joined the household, it needed to be something much more ambitious, so Laura and her father designed and built the shed shown here.

Looking out over a well-kept vegetable garden at the front, the shed is probably one of the grandest you'll ever see, bearing more than a passing resemblance to a Japanese temple, with its large, bright red double doors and wide slate roof swooping over the timber walls. Laura even asks herself, "Has this building gone beyond being a 'shed'?"

Originally meant as storage for animal feed, the shed has exceeded Laura's expectations and resembles a Japanese temple.

above The miniature stallions lead a good life. Their stables form a part of the shed, and their paddock is alongside.

opposite above A canoe is stored on the rafters above the garden room. The wooden steps up to the loft are on a pulley system so they can be lifted out of the way.

inset and opposite right The chickens roost in the coop next to the small kitchen. Two wooden flaps in the dividing wall allow Laura to collect the freshly laid eggs.

It contains a stable for the horses, with a paddock alongside, a chicken coop for two roosters and the chickens, and a simple living space. Laura also decided to incorporate a small kitchen, where she could wash pots, make coffee, and clean and store eggs. Two wooden flaps in the wall dividing the hen house from the kitchen are an ingenious way for her to reach the eggs laid in the coop next door.

Overlooking the forest at the back of the property is the spacious living area, with enormous windows open to the air but covered with mesh to keep out the biting insects. A well-worn wicker sofa and chairs command the view at one end, with a dining table and chairs at the other. This is a social space, somewhere to relax and cool off in the cool breezes off the marshes.

Wooden steps on a pulley system, which lifts them up out of the way when the space is needed for social gatherings, lead up to the soaring open roof. At present, the loft is used primarily for storage—resting over two of the wooden beams is an old wooden canoe—but that could very easily change in the future.

Paddy has four sheds, all of them featured in this book (see also pages 74–5, 168–9, and 180–1), but this one is important to Paddy because she and Gilly, who was the love of her life, built it together. Sadly, Gilly has since died.

Overlooking a cricket pitch, this sweet little potting shed, built for purpose, is tucked away at the end of Paddy's garden in rural Suffolk, England. Painted a soft sea-blue-green, with a contrasting bargeboard and window trims, it looks completely at home in this gardener's garden. Plum, pear, and apple trees, as well as looming mature trees, are all around, but the tall trees cast so much shadow over the flourishing vegetable garden that drastic action may need to be taken to let in more light.

Paddy loves birds, certainly not cats, and she has fixed a bird-box under the shed eaves to entice the next spring visitors. Inside, the shed is full of the usual gardening tricks of the trade, from buckets, tools, netting, and plant pots to seed trays and packets, garden string, beanpoles, and pea sticks. There is even a pile of the card middles from toilet rolls that Paddy has collected, which she uses to protect delicate seedlings from slugs and snails.

As well as using the shed for storage, Paddy creates new life here, nurturing the seeds that she has sown in homemade compost, for later planting out in the vegetable patch.

right Painted green and rust-red, and with a bird-box waiting for the next visitor, this pretty shed conceals a whole raft of gardening equipment.

"This is where magic happens, in the warmth and with a slight smell of creosote..."

Chapter 6

Sheds **for working**

Many of the women whose sheds are featured in this book are working women, and what they do in their shed is how they make their living. They may be painters, sculptors, makers, or growers. However, the work done by the women in this chapter does not fall into those categories. These women work from home or, more correctly, as near to home as their shed can be. Their shed is their office, either full time or part time, and with this shortest of commutes, there are also environmental and economic benefits.

Going to work, taking a journey from the mundane, to a place that's a cocoon, a refuge—maybe with "Private, do not disturb" on the door, maybe with the cell phone left in the kitchen—is therapeutic in itself. In the shed, work can be focused and efficient; it can be left and returned to without disruption—the pen stays where it's put. In a corner, a sofa or an armchair can provide a comfortable retreat for those catching-up moments when the mind needs a little distance from, and perspective on, the job in hand. There is, though, a need for structure and self-discipline, not to get distracted by domestic "to do" lists, or whatever is outside the window.

In the shed, the hours are your hours, to pass however you choose, with only you looking over your shoulder. And when something goes particularly well, no one's looking if you jump up and do the Happy Dance! Working in the shed need not be lonely though—if the phone or internet signal is strong enough, we are still connected to others.

Jenny is outnumbered. Her north Norfolk house is full of males... her partner and their three sons, to be precise. Her shed, on the other hand, is a man-free zone, and it's the only place where she can leave her work on her desk without it being moved around, or put down a pen knowing that it will still be there at the end of the day.

After leaving the teaching profession, Jenny now works as a plantswoman. Her tidy desk looks out onto the vegetable garden surrounded by leafy trees, creating a magical place to be and to work. But her shed is not just a workspace. It's also a bar, a shrine, a retreat, but, above all, a woman's space. It has an old-fashioned cottage feel about it, with its pale green and white walls almost covered by various treasures, from vintage plates and platters to pictures and photographs. Even the back of the door is decorated with bunches of herbs, dried leaves, and the odd postcard or two. There is a small bar in the corner, with her choice of tipple, and glasses at the ready on top of a shelf.

Jenny makes effective use of mirrors, in the vegetable garden as well as in her shed. Inside, they serve to increase the sense of space and introduce an air of mystery. Dotted around the garden, they reflect light and color, and the two on the outside of the door, together with the painting, turn the tiny veranda into an outdoor room.

Strings of fir cones and shells from the beach festoon the veranda, where two mismatching rustic chairs bid visitors welcome, to sit down with Jenny and, perhaps, relax with one of her favorite tipples.

above Mirrors and a picture on the door, comfortable chairs on the veranda, and strings of shells and fir cones hanging from the eaves suggest that this shed is a woman's space. As well as being her place of work as a plantswoman, the shed is also Jenny's escape from a male-dominated household.

opposite Simply furnished and with personal treasures lining the walls, the shed has an old-fashioned, cottagey feel about it.

Kathy's shed was built as an office, squeezed in at the end of the long, narrow garden (yard) of her urban home in Somerset, England. Painting it a soft pale blue on the outside has taken it from being a run-of-the-mill garden feature to something rather special.

The shed is full but the storage has been so well organized that it is still a clear and efficient space in which to work. As well as Kathy's desk, complete with computer, there are filing cabinets with the printer on top, cubbyholes for books and files, and a cupboard.

What distinguishes this office space most from those in the corporate world is the comfy sofa, and the very pretty wire table and chairs just outside. It is clearly a multifunctional space, designed and furnished to meet many needs, including periods of rest and renewal, which contribute to the balance of the working day. This lack of formality is deliberate on Kathy's part. Her work as an independent, educational psychologist means working with clients face to face, but that happens elsewhere. Her shed is emphatically a client-free zone.

Editing reports comes easily in this very peaceful, personal space. In the winter, the shed is warm and cozy; in summer, Kathy can fling the doors wide open, to breathe in the fresh air and listen to the sounds of nature. For Kathy, as for many women, this proximity to nature that her shed allows is essential to her well-being.

When Kathy wants a break from the computer, she can sit on the sofa with a cup of tea. And when she feels tired, she can lie on the sofa and take a refreshing nap before going back to work! Rosie, her dog, is a constant companion. She follows Kathy down the path from the house at the start of every working day and curls up on the rug. Her gentle snores are soothing background noise as Kathy works.

The pictures pinned above the desk are all of family, friends, and the places Kathy has loved best on her travels. If her brain needs a rest, she gazes at them and drifts off with her memories.

"Right now it's raining and the sound of the raindrops on the roof is soothing and makes me feel cocooned in my own little workspace."

left The graveled area, with the wire table and chairs and plants all around, distances the shed from the house, so that domestic demands are forgotten. With the doors flung wide open, Kathy feels much closer to nature.

For something so tiny, **Melanie's** unassuming wooden shed has given birth to, and nurtured, an incredible number of creative activities. It's been used as a central office for a major dance festival, as a performance space, and as a meeting space. But, most important of all, it is Melanie's space where she can shut herself away and think and create.

Melanie is a freelance interdisciplinary artist, and her work involves a lot of traveling away from her Glastonbury home in Somerset, England. When she had her twin boys, she had to rethink the way she worked and lived her life. She needed to be apart from the house but also close to her children. The solution was to convert the small 1950s shed at the end of the garden (yard) into an office and studio.

She wanted the space to have that traditional quality of a "shed at the bottom of the garden where dad disappeared to for a smoke and a read." To that end, she kept all the original design and layout, just adding a desk, a work area, and a few shelves.

Much closer to the house stands a replica of a Stourbridge leper chapel that Melanie made for one of her projects. In spite of its ecclesiastical inspiration, the structure has a "shed-like" quality but it's also rather surreal, in an Alice in Wonderland kind of way, on account of its small scale. It has no particular use other than as a thing of beauty.

left To all intents and purposes, this diminutive replica of a medieval chapel–a surreal addition to the garden–is a shed.

opposite Set against a wooden fence and with mature trees all around, this unassuming shed merges into the background at the bottom of the garden.

"This year my children left home and now I no longer use the shed as a studio. But it's not been rejected; it's just transforming. Its next manifestation will be as a massage room."

Gill moved from her home in Norfolk, England, with its enormous studio (see pages 40–1), to the middle of a Suffolk village, where she has three sheds. The first, situated at the end of the vegetable garden, is sturdy and weatherproof, making it ideal for storage. Here, Gill keeps everything from gardening and home improvement tools to a few personal things belonging to her daughter. The second is an old flint building, Gill's studio, where she intends to take up painting again one day, and to make sculptured lights (see page 41).

The third shed, featured here, is an office. Gill's dear departed friend Caroline, whose shed it was before, built it for herself as a place to write novels and plays away from the house. Gill, too, has adopted the shed as a place of writing. Her plan is to write in the mornings and garden in the afternoons. Mostly, that is what she does. However, she can drift off and is often to be found gazing out of the window, deep in thought, at her flint studio shed.

Between the two sheds is what Gill laughingly calls "the garden," more a jungle of weeds, and the pond. Beyond is her vegetable garden, over which she is proud to have some measure of control.

Gill felt no desire to change the colors that Caroline had originally chosen. The pretty light gray-green on the walls and the contrasting lilac on the floor give an overall impression of light, helped along by the tall double doors, window, and roof light. An African rug woven from recycled plastic in reds and turquoise brightens up the floor.

As well as there being memories of Caroline here, there are those of Gill's father, too. Among the many books in the shed is his collection of art books.

Gill moved here just over a year ago and, as she freely admits, everything, including the books, is still waiting for some order to be imposed. She is adamant she will get around to it "... if only I can stop myself opening the pages, rummaging, remembering."

above Gill sat at this desk to write the pages for this book.

opposite As the shed has its back to the house, it's easier for Gill to focus on her writing. In summer, the trellis on the side of the shed is covered with clematis, one large and purple, the other a delicate blue.

"What being in here does is bring back that very pleasurable childhood memory of making a den: draping blankets over chairs and arranging buttercups in a jam jar then just lying there blissfully till (with any luck) somebody says it's teatime."

166 Sheds for working

Standing in dense undergrowth, this old trailer (caravan) in Suffolk can hardly be seen from beyond the garden (yard). It has settled into the bushes and trees. Patched up and held together over the years by a friend who nailed planks of wood over the critical bits of disintegration and sealed off the holes in the roof, this place is a testimony to 1950s construction. **Sarah** laughs dryly as she comments, "I probably didn't need to put that sign by the door saying, 'No Door to Door Salespeople.'"

Although rough around the edges, with rusty fittings and a covering of moss, the trailer is a dry place to work. Sarah is a cartoonist and her justification to the world out there is that she uses the old trailer for coming up with ideas for her cartoons and then drawing them. However, she admits this isn't strictly true—she does most of her drawing and creating on the kitchen table, amid household clutter. When she escapes to the trailer and closes the door behind her, she enters an oasis of solitude, where domestic chores and the pressures of daily life are forgotten.

Dappled light from the large window is thrown onto her writing desk. Sarah has all she needs here to work, as well as some comforts, such as a samovar for making tea and an electric heater. When she chooses this space over the kitchen table, she is able to think and imagine in peace. However, try as she might to settle down to work, she is invariably distracted, finding other more important tasks to do, such as

"sharpening old pencil stubs, laying them in order of length, dusting the windows with a hanky, sifting through old photographs and letters, daydreaming…" Only when these are completed can she gather her wits and come up with an inspired idea for her next cartoon!

opposite and inset Bruised and battered, the old trailer seems to be fighting a losing battle with nature, but inside all is still dry and cozy.

Three "generations" of friends have owned this house, which backs onto a cricket pitch at the end of a long Suffolk lane. Each of these women has left her mark, not least on the sheds that they have built.

The oldest is the tin shed, set in the orchard and built by Lizzy (see pages 180–1). Cee had the boat house built (see pages 98–9) when she lived here, and Gilly's potting shed (see pages 154–5) and studio were put up by Paddy and her partner Gilly together.

The shed featured here is **Paddy's**, where she writes poetry. Her work is mainly political, sometimes comic, but it also speaks of love and loss. It was originally Gilly's studio, where she painted and drew until she became too ill to continue. But her sketches, watercolors, and pastels remain pinned to the wall, holding precious memories of Gilly's skill and vibrancy.

The clever use of paint, inside and out, reflects Gilly's and Paddy's love of mixing colors, to wonderful effect. The doors, windows, and clapboard walls are dark blue, but when the doors are opened out, they reveal a harmonious pastel mix of green and pink, which bring the interior to life. The windows inside are painted the same pastel green, complementing Paddy's rustic chair. Rich cream paneled walls are a warm and neutral backdrop for Gilly's work, and the wooden floor is softened with rugs.

right and opposite
Gilly and Paddy used an inspired mix of colors to decorate the shed both inside and out. The artworks by Gilly are treasured mementoes, and the cream of the paneled walls allows them to stand out and be fully appreciated.

"Gilly's studio was where she used to draw and paint, collecting around her beautiful and useful things. When she started to forget how to do things, she would stand outside, arms clasped around her, looking in—just as her work was beginning to flourish. I watched her, helpless, as she grieved for things she could no longer reach."

Diney's shed, in a corner of her small garden (yard) in Kew, London, is primarily her office where she sees psychotherapy clients. It is a minimalist space, absolutely pristine, with just two armchairs, a bookcase, three tiny tables, and white-painted walls. For those seeking help dealing with life's challenges, it is just right.

For Diney, the shed is also a memorial to two dear friends. Elizabeth, a gardener, first suggested to Diney that she build her therapy shed and where it should go. And Len, a local builder, who knew all there was to know about his trade, made it a reality. Both have since died but the shed is a constant and welcome reminder of their friendship.

As you approach the six-sided shed, with its porthole window, it appears to be in some idyllic grove, far from its urban home. Painted white inside and out, it has a serene atmosphere, perfect for client and therapist. The design was inspired by a small, white chapel on a minute island in the bay in Malia, Crete. As the finishing touch, Diney wanted a dome for her shed, just like the chapel, which would be visible from the outside. Perhaps not surprisingly, the proposal was thrown out by the local planning department. Len then devised a large circular skylight instead, which lets in lots of daylight, and tiny blue lights were installed around it, to create a pretty effect at night.

left Minimalist inside and out, Diney's shed is where she sees her psychotherapy clients. With no decoration to distract, the space is perfect for the task.

Down a long path and partially obscured by the bushes, this shed, in Whitstable on the Kent coast in England, is a writer's room, a retreat, a guest room.

When **Frankie** and her partner **Diane** moved into their house, the wooden shed was already in the garden (yard)—the previous owner had kept a model railway locked inside. The shed's Mediterranean-blue paneled walls are now collaged with photographs and pictures of favorite places—Kaikoura in New Zealand, Derek Jarman's Kent cottage, Dartmoor in Devon—and cards and portraits of inspirational people—the musician Patti Smith, the poet Mahmoud Darwish, the writer Grace Paley, Frankie's mother, and many others.

Frankie has just finished writing her first novel at the desk and has started on another. In between times, she takes advantage of the peaceful atmosphere and daydreams on the bed or sits in the wicker chair, rereading favorite books. In summer, she sometimes sleeps here, and the last thing she sees before closing her eyes is the Milky Way twinkling in the sky.

Friends love to visit, often staying over, perhaps writing or painting during the day. They, too, appreciate the peace that soothes and the color that lifts the spirits. On balmy nights, laughter, music, and politics fill the air as they all gather outside.

Nature is literally on the doorstep. At the door, bees and butterflies flit through honeysuckle, buddleia, and brambles; birds patter across the roof; the rain thrums down; plums drop onto the shingle. It's a space to enjoy silent solitude or to share with friends over cups of tea.

Frankie knows how lucky she is to have a place to live, to be able to write, to be a human being, a woman with a shed:

above Frankie's half-hidden shed was home to the previous owner's model railway but she has turned it into a much more adaptable space—it's a writer's room, guest room, and retreat all rolled into one.

"Once, on a creative writing course at a wonderful Arvon Foundation centre, I enthused to an organizer about the wooden sheds dotted around the grounds. Peaceful, empty, except for a table and chair, with windows onto gardens, they're perfect for writing, concentrating, dreaming.

'I'm inspired,' I said. 'I've decided to get one of my own, one day.'

He looked at me askance and laughed.

'They're bloke's things, sheds,' he said. 'Sheds are for blokes, Frankie.'

It was one of those moments: there you are going about your life, thinking of yourself as a human being, a person among equals, and, wham! you're stymied by someone else's view of you—a prisoner of gender."

above and inset The clear coastal light floods through the windows, bringing the Mediterranean-blue walls to life. Photographs postcards, and cuttings, pinned directly to the walls almost haphazardly, add to the informality of the space.

Chapter 7

Sheds **for builders**

The motivation for women to build their own shed includes commitments to recycling, limited budgets, or just the challenge of doing it for themselves. Their sheds are part of a vision of sustainability. Recycling, reusing, and reinventing guide women's designs as they take care of the Earth's resources and do their bit to restrain the consumerist world. The recycled shed uses railway tie (sleepers), windows, scraps of corrugated tin, things that other people have thrown away, and these women know where to find them. They have an eye for foraging at auctions, in dumpsters (skips), and at yard (car boot) sales. They also know who to ask for help.

Taking advantage of their knowledge and experience, and with an eye for using what is around them, these women have created unusual, innovative buildings and sheds for themselves and others. By seeing the value in what already exists around them, they can make aesthetically fantastic and quirky buildings.

Caring for the environment and being energy efficient, such as having good insulation, wood-burning stoves, and green "living" roofs, are important concerns to them. Many self-builders also choose to use traditional materials and techniques.

An existing shed can be an inspiration. Stored in the memory, it can be a template for your desires, to be used at a later date.

above Cacti, lined up like sentries, give interest to the plain whitewashed wall of the shed. The spider web, which Christie fashioned out of iron rods and wire, is an intriguing decoration.

Two hours north of Melbourne, Australia, on the Broken River, lies the town of Benalla. **Christie**, an artist and a sculptor, lives on the outskirts of the town and is in the final stages of building her beautiful eco-house.

A corrugated iron shed in the garden (yard) grew as the house grew, becoming a refuge from the heat, a store, and a workshop, as well as her home for a time. Its contents, covered in dust, are in a state of limbo, waiting to be moved into the house when it is ready.

Christie now rents a house in town, where she has these two sheds. One is used for storage of various odds and ends and for

drying herbs and prunings that she collects to use in her art. Outside, an impressive collection of cacti almost obscures the whitewashed wall.

Cacti and succulents are perfect plants for Christie to grow. She is passionate about gardening but the climate is often very unforgiving—at the time of my visit, it was midsummer and the only green grass to be seen was at the nearby golf course. The jewel-like flashes of red, green, pink, and white in the surrounding trees are unsurprisingly not from plants but raucous cockatoos, parrots, and rosellas.

above Containers of cacti and succulents—plants of choice in this uncompromising climate—are given height by being displayed on sawn-off logs.

"There is even plenty of room to store all of my tools and the many other 'materials' that I collect for the creative projects that these sheds inspire."

Leaning against the soft gray corrugated tin of the second shed are rustic wooden steps, which act as a display case for Christie's extensive collection of drought-loving succulents. This shed is much larger but there's nothing inside it as yet. Christie plans to turn it into a den, sculpture studio, and workshop, complete with welding equipment, so that she can transform all manner of recycled materials into pieces of art. She also plans to use it for making costumes for her performance art and creating furniture out of recycled materials, as well as repairing pieces that have seen better days.

The shed's generous size may mean that it will end up being divided into two, to be shared between Christie and her daughter Aeisha, who envisions a hangout for her and her friends. Inevitably, the two spaces will take on different personalities.

left The corrugated tin of the second shed makes a pleasing backdrop to a display of potted succulents, some of them on the steps of a ladder.

Paddy has a number of sheds, four of which are featured in this book (see also pages 74-5, 154-5, and 168-9). Each of them has a different role to play in her life, and each has its own history, filled with meanings and memories. The tin shed featured here in her garden (yard) in rural Suffolk, England, is the oldest but, in spite of its ramshackle appearance and the wind blowing its roof off one violent winter, Paddy still holds it very dear. Pitched and patched, it's a unique shed that her dear friend Lizzy made for her.

This was Lizzy's first attempt at building a shed, which she did from corrugated tin and two-by-two timber. Her father showed her how to make a half-lap joint and a straight cut with a handsaw by finding what he called "the sweet spot," where the blade moves easily. Lizzy sourced the tin from the local auction sale ground. On the way back, it cut through the binder twine holding it on the van roof and it blew off in a high wind. Not to be daunted, Lizzy retrieved the tin and started on her serial shed-building mission (see pages 46-7 and 182-3).

Paddy has often thought about replacing it with something solid that will withstand the elements, perhaps with a veranda to catch the last of the evening light, but will she? She has a huge amount of affection for this weathered and rusty shed, tucked away among the trees and bushes. It is also still very useful, holding all those bulky possessions that Paddy can't bear to part with and wouldn't know where else to store.

The lives of Paddy and her friends are so closely entwined that if one of them decides to sell up and move, the likelihood is that it will be to another friend's house nearby. As they move, they change, add, and protect the old and the treasured possessions that have been left behind.

right It looks as though a puff of wind could blow this old tin shed down, but Paddy loves it and will keep it going for another year.

"The old tin shed stands—and will probably do so until the next friend arrives."

West meets East in this very English setting behind a converted
forge, which is now **Rosie's** home. Roses and potted bamboo flank
the handmade shed in the garden (yard) of her Suffolk, England,
home. Made from recycled wood and corrugated tin, it sits
comfortably in its setting by a pond in the midst of mature trees.

Like Paddy's old tin shed on pages 180–1, Rosie's shed was
built by their mutual friend Lizzy. She positioned it so the
afternoon sun would stream in through the windows, and she
sourced all the materials from local auctions, Emmaus charitable
communities in France, and reclamation yards. Raised on stilts to
create height, the shed had enough room underneath for storing
boats and wood. Originally, it was lived in but now it's a workshop
and used for storage. While listening to the radio, Rosie renovates
furniture—chairs both on the floor or hanging from hooks wait for
her attention. A small but efficient wood-burning stove makes this
an all-year-round workshop.

An adjoining potting shed was built at the same time and in the
same style. Rosie painted both of them black, and they look

"To some people, this would be simply a wooden shed but to many of the world's poorest it would be the ultimate in luxury. To me, it is a contribution to my life by people I care about."

stunning against the luscious green of the trees. In the summer vibrant red roses climb up and over the black corrugated tin roofs, creating wonderful contrasts and a sense of drama.

Another friend, Mick, built the veranda. Rosie recalls how he measured and measured because he cared so much about the proportions, and how he covered the wooden deck with chicken wire because he worried that she might slip. Lined along the front of the veranda is a family of Chinese stone dogs, adding to the oriental feel.

Meanwhile, friends Bob and Barbara gave Rosie a quince tree for making quince vodka and mostarda di Venezia, a mustard-flavoured quince paste. Planted at one end of the shed, the quince now yields a hearty crop every year.

Lizzy is an inveterate builder, and two of the earlier sheds she created for friends are also featured in this chapter (see pages 180–1 and 182–3). She has been building sheds for twenty years now, and the one shown here is hers, looking completely at home in her garden (yard) near Diss, in Norfolk, England.

Not one to be outdone, Lizzy saw my shed with its veranda (see pages 40–1) and had to have one of her own! She started off by drawing a modest design on paper the following morning. She had already acquired a batch of old telephone poles that were being replaced on the hill nearby. By the evening, she had a man and a digger ready to start work. The combination of wishing to use all the poles and having all the help and equipment she needed led to a much bigger design than she had originally intended.

The telephone poles are like stilts, and the shed is fixed to them, suspended a couple of feet above the ground. Lizzy has used the space created to store building materials, a double kayak, and a French duck-shooting boat that she made some years ago.

Lizzy is an expert recycler, with an unerring eye for the quirky and the beautiful. She had a wood-burning stove made for the shed out of a recycled gas bottle. She found the windows and the basin while traveling around the Sierra Nevada mountains in Spain and drove them back in her van. The timber and cladding are from closer to home, acquired at the local auction. A solid door, from Eastern Europe, opens out onto a light, open space, where Lizzy composes and writes, and her band rehearse.

inset The chalet-style shed has been made completely out of recycled materials.

far right The blue of the door and windows has been picked out in the basketweave decoration hanging on the wall.

It has long been **Maggie's** dream to have a room of her own—somewhere to paint, write, and simply retreat from the world whenever she wanted. Implicit in her vision was to use recycled materials wherever possible and for the structure to be true to its setting.

All in all, Maggie's shed in her Derbyshire, England, garden (yard) is a testament to creativity and resourcefulness. With the help of her friend Brian, she built this delightful hexagonal structure, with its jolly green door and windows, from whatever they could find, which, in part, dictated the design.

In the end, the shed has turned out to be more or less entirely recycled. It boasts reclaimed slates, a Velux window from a friend's roof, windows from her own house when she replaced them, and a reclaimed oak floor, together with as much reused roof and floor insulation as they could muster. The slate roof, meanwhile, was made from a friend's castoffs.

A single solar panel provides more than enough power for light and music, and possibly, in the future, for running a darkroom. The shed is deceptively spacious, and there's room for a wood-burning stove, making it a comfortable place to be in the depths of winter. As luck would have it, the college where she works and her neighbors were getting rid of pieces of furniture, and Maggie has found a welcoming home for it all in her studio.

The bench immediately outside and the shed walls are made from railway ties (sleepers). Even these chime in with Maggie's wish for her shed to be true to its setting—a railway line runs past the bottom of the garden, and trains speed along it.

"Creating, sourcing, building took over two years and I feel I am starting to have the confidence to call it my studio."

"It's amazing stuff but, oh cob, why do I love thee? Because, if I'm honest... it makes me feel good. I get a tingle down my spine when I slap squidgy, sticky mud into a wall or gently shape and smooth it around a window or shelf."

Cob building, a traditional method of construction that uses a mix of clay, sand, straw, and water, is how **Kate** makes her living, and she is in constant demand to build sheds, even entire homes, from this natural material.

Arguably, cob is the most environmentally friendly building material there is. It makes inexpensive yet beautiful structures that are long-lasting and nontoxic, and also meet modern building regulations and planning requirements. Cob homes are also cheap to maintain, having just a fraction of normal heating costs.

Kate's tiny old house was extended with a cob and straw-bale structure, which has more than doubled the size of her home, and there is hardly any need for additional heating. She's also given it a thatched roof, to match that of the house

The house is set in a remote part of Norfolk, England, on the inland stretch of waterways known as the Broads. From here, when she's not building for others, she and her partner Charlie run cob-building courses for people from all over the world, many of whom have never done work of this sort before. Students have built a pizza oven under a canopy, and are currently working on a new cob shed that will eventually be her office. The design is centered on a reclaimed window. It will have complementary French doors, as well as a living sedum roof. The outside will be rendered in lime, like the house.

Kate is very clear about why she works with cob—she finds the whole experience sensual, meditative, and completely enjoyable. The cob molds easily into whatever shape she chooses, such as a staircase, a bed, or a bench. But the best bit is the end result: a building that's breathable, cheap, and sculptural.

opposite and above Clay and straw, the raw materials used in the traditional art of cob building, can be seen clearly in this work in progress for Kate's new office. The design is centered on the reclaimed window, which is already in situ.

opposite below The shapely pizza oven, set under a canopy, is also built from cob.

Julie's shed is a cob house in the garden (yard) of her Norfolk, England, home. Kate, the cob builder (see pages 188–9), followed Julie's wishes. The building, a squat roundhouse, is eco-friendly and suits its surroundings and purpose—people come here to drum, dance, and tell stories.

Clay, the main raw material, was dug from the garden, and straw bales were brought from a neighboring farm. The clay was then mixed with sand by naked feet in what has come to be called "the cob dance." The cob, which forms the walls, was lovingly molded by hand, with help from volunteer "cobbers," keen to learn this natural method of building.

Growing over the conical roof of this "hobbit house" are sedum plants, creating a mat of vivid green that contrasts beautifully with the golden, lime-washed exterior. Above the gothic-arched door, panels of stained glass let in the light. In summer the sun streams through them, spilling colors onto the cool earth walls and floor. As the colder evenings draw in, the space is lit by candlelight, and heat, which the cob walls absorb and retain, is provided by the wood-burning stove. The flue is a quirky and irregular-sculpted "hat."

left The quirky, orange-painted flue makes a compelling focal point in the drumming shed. The uneven cob walls reflect their hand-made nature.

opposite above and below Julie's squat "hobbit house" is built from cob, with sedum plants covering the conical roof. Round, crisscross windows, with uneven sills, have been set into the golden lime-washed walls. The elegant recycled gothic doors contribute further to the structure's eco credentials.

"This is a sacred space and meeting place filled with a wonderful spiritual energy. A garden house of healing and laughter in which to sit and journey or meditate and feel uplifted and at peace."

On the outskirts of a small village near Le Mans in northwest France and along an unmarked road, you will find **Colette's** beautiful house, La Rubrie, and its *dépendances*—the sheds.

There is a barn with a beaten earth floor, saved from dilapidation by restoring the roof and the bargeboards. Friends lent a hand, and her father made the enormous sliding doors. Inside, Colette stores bicycles, agricultural machinery, wooden boards, doors, and windows that might come in useful one day.

The small, pretty barn, closer to the house, was tackled next. The building had been divided into a piggery and, possibly, a cowshed, complete with an old manger, but this part of the building had partially collapsed and, as a result, became known affectionately as "the ruins." After clearing away stones and rubble, Colette rebuilt it. Later, she was able to achieve her desire to expose the splendid half-timbering that had been hidden by boarding. Glass was installed between the timbers to let in light. Today, in one half of the building she keeps wood; in the other, tools. The

above left and insets Different aspects of the small, pretty barn, with the original structure clear to see.

above right The half-timbering of the restored large barn, hidden beneath boarding for years, can once more be fully appreciated.

above left Even the outside toilet looks welcoming, with a cutout heart in the door!

inset Colette rebuilt the large barn, which is now used for storage.

below left The first building you see upon entering the property is this intriguing round-ended shed. Once the pigeon house, it now stands empty.

below right Grapevines meander across the walls of the small barn, which form part of the lean-to greenhouse.

right Colette's collection of hand-blown Dame Jeanne green glass bottles.

manger has been given a new lease of life as storage for salvaged traditional roof tiles, in anticipation of a future building project

Not far from these two storage areas, there were a further two buildings until Colette filled in the gap between them, put in an old door, and created her above-ground "cellar." Here she keeps her collection of hand-blown Dame Jeanne glass bottles, which she fills with the walnut wine that she makes every summer.

Colette also has a workshop. The timber structure was built by a local carpenter, assisted by Colette's friends who put in lathes and added the roof of traditional local tiles made of terra-cotta. It is Colette's dream to turn the space into a ceramics workshop but that will have to wait until she has bought a kiln and installed heating. For the time being, it is used to store apples and garden furniture—and have parties. The "courtyard" of the workshop opens to the elements, and Colette dries her linen there in the wind, even in the middle of winter.

right Everything has its place in the shed, with nails and screws stored in glass jars on open shelves, and tools hung from hooks in the wall. The multi-drawer wooden chest contains even more tools.

opposite left The baskets hanging from the beams add personality to the space.

opposite right Cobwebby boots are the only things in the shed that appear neglected!

Claire's shed by the side of her Suffolk, England, home was once a garage but she converted it a few years ago and has never looked back. It is crammed full of stuff, but if you peer closely, you soon realize that none of it is random—there is a place, a shelf, a hook for everything.

Claire is a life coach, an environmental university tutor, and a gardener. What's more, when it comes to house maintenance, she does it all herself. With such a full and busy life, systems are essential to her but she also finds them hugely enjoyable.

She has come to the conclusion that a large, unavoidable part of her life, and everybody else's for that matter, is taken up with caring for things,

"You won't see my shed featured in a magazine, but its workspace, its storage, and its organization are important to me because they support good maintenance. This, in turn, creates a home environment vibrant with unhindered creativity, productivity, and fulfillment."

such as our homes, gardens (yards), and cars, not to mention for ourselves. For a woman who thrives on order and efficiency, this isn't as dull as it sounds. Claire firmly believes that good maintenance oils the wheels that allow great things to happen without hindrance. Efficient maintenance requires that well-kept tools are to hand when needed, in a well-designed space.

With this purely functional shed, Claire has certainly achieved this. She keeps a lot of her tools in a made-to-measure, multi-drawer wooden chest that fits inside a large carpenter's trunk. Many of them are quite old, inherited from her father or grandfather. This makes them even more enjoyable to use, especially with their lovely wooden handles. Screw-topped glass jars, lined up neatly on wooden shelves, reveal their contents at a glance, while saws, hand drills, and a vice each have their own hook from which to hang. As Claire says, this is a practical shed for practical things, although the baskets hanging from the beams add a decorative touch.

Isa bought this house for the stunning view but also so she could start a new relationship and a new life. The house, which is in Le Sarthe, northwest France, had been empty for a long time and it needed more than a lick of paint to make it habitable. The sheds, too, had to be taken in hand and restored. Isa brought much of her past with her when she moved, and those things that she couldn't bear to part with out of nostalgia needed to be stored somewhere safe.

Fortunately, Isa is a very practical woman, completely at home with a chainsaw and the many other tools she has used for the renovations. She has strengthened the four walls of her largest barn and given it a new roof. And so begins a new cycle of storing and sheltering. Meanwhile, the old cowshed is now full of firewood and bundles of sticks, ready to be burned in the fireplace during winter. The defunct well nearby has been brought back to life and provided with a new pump, making it easier to take care of the garden that Isa has planted with fruit and vegetables.

inset The shed within a shed, where Isa keeps her tools and all those things that might come in useful one day.

With another barn she has created a shed within a shed, where she stores her tools. "This might be useful, you never know…" is a phrase that could be justly applied here. There are drawers full of hinges, doorknobs, hooks, and more. Taking advantage of the wall space, she has fixed a plywood board and from it, hanging on hooks or resting on nails, is an impressive collection of spanners of various sizes, neatly graded by size. Everything has its proper place.

above, right, and inset
Roses clambering their way up the rough stone walls of the renovated barn and a windowbox of pelargoniums at the cobwebby window make a charming picture. The wooden fence next to the window conceals water butts.

A new staircase leads upstairs, where, time permitting, Isa sits by the window to do some basket making.

With apparently no limits to her do-it-yourself skills, she has also built a chicken coop. With its timber-lapped walls and terra-cotta-tiled roof, it mimics the local architecture perfectly.

left and inset Not content with finishing all her renovation work, Isa then embarked on building a chicken coop. Made of local timber and terra-cotta tiles, it looks right at home with all the other buildings.

thinking about **a shed**

This list of questions will, I hope, serve as inspiration for any woman dreaming about having a shed of her own.

What is my ideal?

What would I like to create in my life?

What are my wildest dreams?

What are my passions?

What are my motivations for having a shed?

What resources do I have?

What external resources are available?

What is stopping me from having the shed I want?

What can I do to overcome physical constraints?

What's holding me back?

What are the limiting factors?

How can I change limits into advantages and possibilities?

What strategies can I put in place to support me in getting my shed?

What is my timescale?

Are there people who can support me?

What could I do differently to achieve my aims and vision?

What blocks are there to my ideas from becoming successful?

Can I recognize my or other people's patterns that hold me back?

What patterns from nature, other people, or different activities would help me with my design?

What patterns in design and building can I replicate or adapt?

I am grateful to Looby Macnamara and her book *Permaculture and People*, which has guided me through my own process in writing this book.

Index

Acknowledgments

I would like to thank the following people who began this journey with me: Lizzy Smith, Mel Wright, and Nicolette Hallett. Great excitement and encouragement to continue and realize the book came from Paddy Tanton and Frankie Green. Paddy has been a support throughout, as has Sarah Guthrie. Nicky Stainton, Mary Muir, and Jan Dungey helped find the first sheds, and Lesley Kershaw was of key importance in helping to send this book out into the world. I also thank the many people who have cheered me on—you know who you are.

Nicolette and I have traveled far and wide to meet women and take photos of their sheds. We have sat in cars, been on flights, got lost and found, worked very well together, and respected each other's expertise and personalities. I want to thank Nicolette for her wonderful photos and the patience sometimes needed when dealing with other human beings—including me!

I would also like to thank family and friends who have been neglected but have supported me throughout.

Last but not least, I would like to thank all the shed owners and builders: Meg Amsden, Claire Appleby, Gail Arnold, Candace Bahouth, Caroline Barry, Anne Belgrave, Maddy Bragar, Rachel Buck, Diney Buirski, Robyn Challis, Sue Chapman, Claude Chouin, Kathy Contaris, Sarah Cook, Kate Edwards, Jenny Elliott, Sarah Evertson, Brenda Figuerido, Jane Frost, Marion Gaze, Jenny Goater, Dee Goddard, Frankie Green, Sarah Guthrie, Nicolette Hallett, Chris Hancock, Helen Hepburn, Bridget Heriz, Bay Heriz-Smith, Kerina Jane, Isabelle Lacroix, Jeanette Lanham, Trish le Gal, Colette Macquin, Johanna W. McKenzie, Marian Meiracker, Dora Atwater Millikin, Kelly Milukas, Catherine Mougne, Tessa Newcomb, Maggie Norman, Jenny Nutbeem, Jude O'Keefe, Elspeth Owen, Christie Phillipson, Maddy Pikarsky, Susan Mohl Powers, Bryn Raven, Julie Reynolds, Helen R, Charlotte Ruse, Christina Ruse, Laura Russell, Meredith Russell, Kathy Scott, Aileen Richmond Shaw, Lindsay Simon, JR Smith, Lizzy Smith, Fiona Strodder, Rosie Squires, Nicky Stainton, Kim Tailor, Paddy Tanton, Melanie Thompson, Jen Toll, Cee Tordoff, Alison Wagstaff, Ann Woolston, Mel Wright, and Chris Wuyts.